STRONG WOMAN ARISEN

Ravenwolf

Copyright © 2023 by The Ravenwolf

All rights reserved. This book or any portion thereof may not be reproduced or used in any manner whatsoever without the express written permission of the publisher except for the use of brief quotations in a book review or the like.

First Paperback Edition: October 2023
ISBN: 979-8-88525-442-7 (print)
Hyperbole Publishing
www.theravenwolf.com

This book is dedicated to Melissa,
the strongest woman with
the most beautiful heart
I've ever known.

Stories of Courage, Strength & Empowerment

She Overcame Everything Meant to Destroy Her 1

I've Never Chosen The Woman I Became, My Path Chose Me Instead. 3

Every Day, She Shows Up 6

She Does What it Takes to Make it Through Today 8

The Independent Women 11

Today I Rise 14

Wait Til You See Who I Become. 16

She's A Warrior. She's You. 18

Watch Me 20

Strong Enough 22

I Fell Apart & Kept Going.. 24

She Refused to Stay Down 26

I'm Not Afraid of the Fire. 28

I've Missed Me. Glad She's Coming Back.................................. 31

I Live Big, Don't Dare Try to Love Me Small............................... 34

I Will Walk Away... 37

I'm a Real Woman.. 39

I Always Find A Way to Get Back Up 42

I'm Proud of Who I Am Today and What It Took to Get Here..... 45

Some Days She Has No Idea How, but Every Day It Still Gets Done 47

Strong Women Aren't Born, We Are Forged in the Fire 51

My Strength Was Born in the Moments I was Forced to my Knees 54

I'll Never Apologize For My Fire 56

She's A Strong Woman with A Soft Heart and Fierce Love 59

Blessed Not Broken 62

But What if You Fly? 64

She Kept Trying, and That Was the Bravest Thing of All 66

They Doubted Me… 69

She's Once in a Lifetime 72

Standing Alone Doesn't Mean I Am Alone. It Means I Am Strong Enough to Handle Things by Myself 74

I am Strong, I am Loved, I am Brave, and I Will Always Be Enough 77

A Strong Woman May Break Down and Cry, But She Will Always Rise Again. 80

You'll Always See the Fire in Her Eyes 82

She has a Heart of Gold in Search of Peace and Love 84

It's My Time to Fly 87

She's Strong and That's Just Who She Is. 90

You are Enough, and You Are Not Alone 93

Don't Worry About Being Beautiful, Be Authentic 95

Even The Strong Need Rest 98

You're Right, I'm A Lot 100

My Passions Burn Brighter Than My Fears	103
The Strong Turn the Pain into Power	105
I Am Not What Happened to Me, I Am What I Choose to Become	107
She is Strong and Chooses to Stay Positive	110
She Finds A Way To Always Get it Done	113
She Became Unstoppable	115
Not Everyone Can Be Strong All The Time	117
My Fiery Heart Will Never Be Tamed	119
A Woman Determined to Rise	121
She Will Rise…	124
She's Not Distant, She Just Refuses to Be Disrespected	126
I Can Overcome Anything	129
I'll Rise Up Better Every Time	132
A Woman Who Can Be Alone is Powerful	136
Today, I Become the Storm	139
The Pain In Her Eyes & The Fire In Her Heart	141
She Never Quit	145
Cheer Me On While I Save Myself	147
Never Mistake Her Quietness For Weakness	150
I'm Worth It- I Always Will Be Worth It	152
I'm Perfectly Flawed, and I Like It	154
Stronger For The Struggle	157
I Fought Hard to Become the Person I Am	160

She's A Butterfly with Bullet Holes In Her Wings…	162
The Deeper The Pain, The Stronger the Wings	164
Behind Every Strong Person Is a Child Who Never Quit Chasing Their Dreams	167
A Strong Woman Picks Up The Pieces	170
My Story is One of Triumph & Tragedy	172
The Price of Becoming Who You Are	175
There is Nothing Greater Than A Self Made Woman	178
Being Remembered For My Strength	180
A Self Renovation	182
My Story	184
I Overcame Everything and Kept Going	187
She Won't Apologize For Her Strength	190
My Scars Tell My Story	**Error! Bookmark not defined.**
I Will Always Be on the Rise	195
She Was a Warm Embrace, His Reminder of Beauty in the World	197
She Fought Her Own Battles	199
The Phoenix	202
The Strongest Women Often Cry Behind Closed Doors	205
The Strength to Love a Broken Woman	207
She Always Finds Her Strength	209
She Does Whatever It Takes	211
I'm Brave Enough to Seek The Life I Want	214
Today, I Rise Again	217

When a Woman Is Silent	219
The Times That Broke Me Showed Me Just How Strong I Could Be	221
I'm a Warrior, Survivor & Fighter	224
Her Strength Is Subtle and True	226
She is a Woman With a Heart of Gold	228
From Broken to Beautiful	231
The Strongest Women Are The Hardest to Catch	234
I Changed It All	236
My Story Chose Me	238
I Got This	240
I Will Not Change Who I am	242
She Will Always Say "I Got This" with Tears in Her Eyes	246
She'll Gather the Best of Her and Then She'll Simply Walk Away	249
Love Yourself Deeply with the Same Passion with Which You Love Others	252
She Will Rise	254
I Will Never Apologize for Who I am	256
Build Her Up	258
She Became Her Own Hero…	260
I Define Me	263
She Was Always Different	265
I'm A Fighter	267
Strong Women Never Settle	269

Her Courage is Her Crown	271
She Learned To Get Back Up	274
She is One of a Kind	276
She's the Strong One	278
She Stopped Holding Out For a Hero	280
The Woman I Am Becoming	282
I Know Who I Am	285
I Choose Me	287
Strong Women Don't Settle	290
I Can Fly	292
Becoming A New Person	295
I Will Rise As The Whole Fire	297
Brave Enough To Be Real	299
I Will Always Be A Fighter	302

Epilogue

She Overcame Everything Meant to Destroy Her

She never wanted to be successful, strong or powerful, she just wanted to be happy.
Along the way to seeking her happiness, life took some turns she never expected.
She didn't choose to become that person that always survived, thrived and overcame…
But she never was given any other choices.
Time and again, she found herself on her knees, battling for her sanity and her survival…
And each time, she managed to emerge from the fire tested but intact.
While she may have once feared the flames of struggle, she was forced to become the fire instead.
When she was at rock bottom, trying to dig her way out of the darkness, the only thing she could cling to was the fire to fuel her ascension…
And so that's just what she did:

She fought bravely, dug deeply and battled furiously to grow and evolve every chance she could.
Everyone counted her out more times than not and each time, she defied the odds and emerged victorious.
That's the thing about a strong woman-
They don't know any other way than to keep going and rising out of the ashes of hardship.
There were stars in her eyes and depths in her soul…
She wasn't ever going to settle for ordinary, lackluster or average.
She was destined for more and every day, in every way, she worked tirelessly to be better than she was the day before.
With a quiet resolve and a determined facade, she endured storms that would overwhelm so many others…
And she took pride in her ability to withstand the obstacles of whatever life threw at her.
She wouldn't ever be perfect, flawless or always put together, but she would be true to herself.
And in a world full of pretense, she celebrated her authentic truths.
She smiled as she knew that she would always be able to say that no matter what, she did it her way.

I've Never Chosen The Woman I Became, My Path Chose Me Instead.

Whatever I needed, whatever life called for- that's who I became.
Whatever role I needed to be, that was who I evolved into...
Mother, sister, partner, friend, mentor, survivor, provider, protector...
I've been each of those and more.
It wasn't about what I ever wanted, but what I needed to do and be.
I always did what I had to do to keep moving forward in my life.
Truth is, I didn't know how I'd make it sometimes, but I always found a way.
I've been the one who everyone looked to for strength, courage and passion, and somehow, I was always able to become what I needed to be.

I won't say it's been easy or painless, because the struggle I fought was almost overwhelming at times... But I made things happen, because that's who I am. I'll never be fearless, flawless or faultless, but I'll always be real, genuine and authentic.
I love with all my heart and I don't do anything halfway.
My soul is filled with passion and I love hard when there's love to be had.
I fill many roles and I have a never ending list of responsibilities, but I've learned I'm capable of conquering anything.
The fires that once threatened to burn me alive now fuel my drive to rise above and fly high.
Maybe my plans don't always work out perfectly and there may have been a time or two when it came off the rails, but I managed to find my way almost every time.
I've provided for and protected those who needed me.
I've loved my people who wanted me.
I've fought for the ones who couldn't do it themselves.
I'm a woman of many talents, qualities and depths...born of the darkest times which forged my ironclad spirit.
But no matter who I've been and what I've done, there's always one part of me that I've needed most: The survivor.
She's the one that kept me going, gave me strength and lifted me up when I fell.

Come what may, she'll always be the part I value most,
For as long as I will ever need her,
She'll always be there.

Every Day, She Shows Up

She'll never tell you that she has everything under control, because most of the time, that's not the case.
She's a delightful combination of strong passionate courage and a brashly hot mess.
She can weather any storm and brave any challenge and come out the other side smiling...
Though some days, it takes all she has just to survive.
You'll never hear her complain about the hand life has dealt, for she's long since accepted her journey and made peace with the choices she's had to make,
Even if they were never really choices to begin with...
Quitting was never an option for her, nor was settling or making do.
No, this sometimes gritty warrior with a heart of gold lives with everything she has and doesn't give up on anyone,
Because she remembers what it feels like to be counted out and watch people walk away from her...

And she's never going to do that to people she cares about.
No, she's the one they can always count on...
She always shows up.
She always fights and keeps going.
She always gives her all, no matter how hard the situation or what has to be done.
There's days that take the breath out of her and times that she doesn't know how she'll find the strength to carry on...
But she does.
She always does.
Maybe she doesn't always take the normal path and perhaps she's a bit of a mess as she stumbles through some things...
But she picks herself up, dusts herself off and slaps a smile on her tired face.
But that's what makes this raw and authentic woman who she is…
A one of a kind warrior spirit who lives her life zealously with love and passion.
If you ever meet this fiery gal, you'll never forget the time when you met her.
She leaves an impression wherever she goes.
Strong, proud and brave...
She does what she has to do every single day...
And that has made all the difference in her journey.
And it's how she keeps going every day...
With a smile on her face and fire in her heart.
Unstoppable, now and always.

She Does What it Takes to Make it Through Today

She made the choice a long time ago to never surrender to the problems and challenges that tried to bring her down.
She never set out to become strong, tough or brave, her story never gave her another option.
She's always done whatever it takes to make it where she's trying to go, but she's never sold her soul or sacrificed her values to reach her goals.
She's not perfect, and she gave up trying to be a long time ago.
She's made her fair shares of mistakes, wrong turns and bad love choices, but that never dissuaded her from pressing forward.
She never asked "why me," she just found a way through the struggles, every time.
She's more than just a simple woman, though you may not know that at first glance.
She's a warrior spirit, with the soul of a dreamer and the heart of a lover...

More than anything, she's been searching for peace and love since the very beginning.
She's always been that person that loves with all her heart-
Herself, her people, her life and perhaps, one day, her "forever person," when he shows up.
She's never questioned the timing of life, she's learned to do the hardest thing of all:
Trust.
Herself, her heart, life's timing, all the things that she should have stopped believing in so long ago, but never did.
She's had her heart broken into a million pieces and she's always been the one to pick up the pieces and put herself back together again...
Each time better and stronger than before.
She's a complex person with simple needs and she's never abandoned her desire to be happy in the things that matter.
She's more than a survivor- though, some days, she felt like that was all she was doing.
Most importantly, she's always kept her fire burning and kept her light shining brightly in her eyes…always believing in herself throughout it all.
Maybe one day she'll rest and take some time for herself, but that time isn't now.
She still has much to do and an entire future full of possibilities...
Falling in love with being alive every day.
Strong, beautiful and free.

One day,
She'll be in love with herself and her life, finally at peace and content-perhaps, even more...
And she can't wait to write the best chapters of her life.

The Independent Women

She's the one that scares off all the men- she is everything they want yet have no idea the truth that lies behind her eyes.
They don't know how to approach her nor what to make of her- she's something rare, beautiful and dangerous to them.
They'll say she is difficult, hard to please or stubborn, but the reality is that she has standards, she's guarded and doesn't settle.
The weaker men will call her the things she isn't because it makes them feel bigger and stronger...
Not because any of it is true.
She doesn't need their approval or permission to be who she wants to be...she never has and never will.
In fact, she'll never need a man, because she's learned she can do anything she needs herself.
She knows that a strong man will not only understand her but will appreciate her as well...
He'll be enraptured by her strength, enamored by her spirit and love her heart...

And that's all she really wants:
Passionate love, soulful connection, and an appreciation of who she is...
But she will never sacrifice her self-respect, her heart or her integrity for anyone.
She won't chase love or attention any more, those were always the pursuits that broke her heart the worse.
If they can't accept her on her terms, she'll just walk away...
She'll never compromise who she is for someone to love her.
The most powerful truth of her is that she doesn't need love, she is content and complete without seeking her love story.
She'll find it when the time is right, but she won't worry about what's meant to be ...because she learned to focus on what she can control- herself.
She knows she isn't easy to love, that she keeps parts of herself guarded, because she's been hurt before and vowed to never again allow someone to destroy her.
Her walls are the highest, but her love is the deepest- she realizes that any man wanting to love her will require patience, empathy and most of all, soulful love.
She's wild and beautiful, not a creature that will ever be tamed or confined.
The one meant for her will get that about her and most of all, he will encourage and support her dreams and desires.

She knows she's not for the faint of heart, her fiery love isn't just for anyone...
but the strongest will find her fire irresistible.
So, until she meets the one who can run with her and loves her burn in only the way her soulmate can,
she'll keep doing what she does best:
Live wild, love hard and always...
She'll enjoy the moments of her life...
Beautiful and free.

Today I Rise

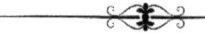

Life never gave her many options on which path to choose.
Just when she made it through one storm, another would roar to life.
There were days she didn't know how she'd survive, pushing through with courage and strength that she didn't know she had.
From the mornings crying in the showers to the quiet nights lying in bed awake, overthinking and exhausted…
But unable to sleep.
Truthfully, she couldn't tell you how she managed to find her way through her days and overcome her battles...
But she always found a way.
To keep going, to rise above and gradually evolve.
Behind her somber eyes lie an incredible depth of brokenness tinged by a lingering sense of sadness...
For all those that left her life, for the things she hadn't done and the heartache that pulled at her soul.
While she was a warrior with a fierce spirit, underneath the steely facade was a soft heart, brimming with love...

Love, in fact, that she was eager to share with those that earned their way into her heart.
Her most intimate places were stashed away behind high walls-
Not to keep others out, but to see who cared enough to tear them down.
If they ever glimpsed into her depths, they were overwhelmed with the gorgeous truths of her deepest secrets and soul love.
But that was the part of her that she reserved for the precious few in her life that she held close and dear.
The world would never know her intimately in that way, for she'd burned those bridges long ago after countless heartbreak and betrayal.
She did what she had to do to protect herself and feel safe.
Her eyes sparkled with a zeal for life and her smile belied her most tender secrets...
So, when she rose in the morning, sometimes soul weary and emotionally exhausted, she would close her eyes, dig deep and stoke the fiery strength of her spirit.
For this remarkable and complex woman was more than just a lover, dreamer and survivor...
She was a warrior who never accepted failure-
With passion in her spirit and fire in her heart, she would face each day bravely, never shrinking from the challenge...
And she would look in the mirror every time and defiantly utter the same fierce promise to herself:
"Today, I rise."

Wait Til You See Who I Become.

All my life, I've been told who I was supposed to be, what I should be doing and all the stuff the world thought I should change.
And for a while, I tried it their way.
It led me down the wrong roads, tore me down and broke my heart countless times over.
With the weight of my life buckling me under, I had to stop doing all the things that broke me...
And start becoming the person I was meant to be.
So that's what I did.
I dug deep, I fought back and started rising from the ashes.
Everyone may have thought I was broken, but I wasn't...
I was healing.
Nothing happens overnight, and my journey back to being whole is a process.
But it's one that is long overdue.
No more excuses, staying down and letting life get the best of me.

No, it's my time now...
To rise above.
To turn my setbacks into a comeback.
To finally become who I knew I could be.
I'm done listening to the critics and everyone who thought they knew what was best for me.
Only I know what I need and deserve,
So that's what I'm fighting for.
I'm standing up strong, proud and resilient.
This is my life and I'm taking charge of it.
I've got greatness coursing in my veins, and it's time I showed the world what I'm truly capable of.
And I know when I start flying high with the wings I've forged from the fires of failure,
They won't know what to make of me...
And they don't have to.
My life, my way.
And this time, I'm aiming for the stars.
Watch me go.
Finally, I am free.

She's A Warrior.
She's You.

She's always been the tough one, the person that everyone knew could handle anything.
They'd marvel at her strength and complimented her fortitude.
What they never knew about this amazing woman is that she never chose to be the way she was...
The hard road of her life never gave her a choice.
It was either keep getting up every time she was knocked down...
Or stay down and give up.
She was not the person that would ever quit.
She didn't know how to stay down.
She was a fighter from the beginning, clawing and scratching her way through the hard times and battling for everything she got.
Given nothing, she became strong because that's how she survived her life.
It wasn't glamorous, appealing or enjoyable, but she did what it took to keep going- keep rising - keep evolving.

There were so many times she just laid in bed and wanted to give up.
Tired of the tears she might cry in the quiet of the night, exhausted from the grind that never relented.
But she wasn't one to shrink from a challenge and she always found a way to make it through, solve the problems, overcome the pain.
She just kept getting up, she kept rising.
She was more than a survivor, she was a warrior.
She was deep of soul and strong of spirit, loving with all her heart and finding her way with brave determination.
She's always had that unbreakable spirit, fire in her eyes and stars in her dreams...
Now, as you look in the mirror, a smile starts to grow as you realize what I've always known.
She's you...and come what may, you'll always rise like a Phoenix.
Today, tomorrow and for always.

Watch Me

She's the one that they can't control, diminish or water down.
She's a fiery spirit with her own opinion, style and voice...
And she won't be silenced or changed by the others who are uncomfortable with her brazen individuality.
She knows who she is because she has paid dearly to become the person she is.
She's failed more times than she can remember, she's made the worst choices and ended up in the wrong places more than she would've liked... but she always did her best to learn from each mistake and grow from every poor decision.
She doesn't regret any of the love she's given or any of the people she's cared about, because she remembered that the people that were meant to be part of her life forever would always be there... the rest were part of her journey to be the best person that she could be.
Sure, they still hurt, those lost friends and even love, sometimes- the heart can't escape that...

But she knew that some pain was part of the growth process...
So that's just what she did:
Kept living, loving and growing every day in every way and never looking back.
There wasn't a challenge she wouldn't tackle or a problem she couldn't solve.
Oh, and those things they said she couldn't do?
Those dreams they lamented that she'd never catch?
Those fears that they said she'd never conquer?
She would do it all with a smile and keep going...
And do even more than she once believed she could.
You could do many things to her,
But you'd never be able to stop her.
And she made sure that when she was gone, you'd never forget her-
The strong woman with a heart of gold and beautiful soul...
She lived without regret, loved with fiery passion and undoubtedly lived her life her way.
Now and for always, she would be unforgettable...
And every bit of unstoppable.

Strong Enough

The world tried to tell me who I should be, how I should act and what I should do...
Only thing was, I wasn't listening.
I've spent all my life listening to the people who thought I should fit into their ideals of how they saw me...
And I'm done with that nonsense.
It never made me happy, so the way I see it, why should I live by what the world thinks when what matters is what makes me happy...
Who I think I should be and what I want to do.
Sure, life isn't always rainbows and sunshine- I'll spend plenty of time doing what I have to do to get through my days...
So why would I want to try to conform to the standards of the world that doesn't want me to stand out, step out and be heard.
Well, I have a voice and I will be heard...
Not because I just want to talk,
But because I have something to say.
See, I'm one of the people that thinks they can change the world:

The misfits, the forward thinkers, the brave ones that want to do more than just accept the status quo.
No, I want to fight for the dreams I have, the people that can't fight for themselves and stand up to the bullies, the greedy and the abusers who hurt others.
So, yeah, I'm going to be different from all the rest.
No, I'm not content with blending in.
I want more.
I am capable of more.
And so are you.
This is my time and I'm much more than just a voice…
I'm fighting for me, you and all of those who are lost and need hope.
Watch what happens when we set the world on fire with the passion of our words and conviction in our hearts.
Anything can be possible if you believe …
And are strong enough to fight for your dreams.
Because I am and always will be strong.
…Ravenwolf strong.
And you are too.
Let's go change the world-
One heart, one dream and one hope at a time.

I Fell Apart & Kept Going

I can't say that I always knew how I'd make it through some days.
Those times when everything seemed to go wrong and anything that could turn upside down would.
Those storms that tore me apart and brought me to my knees would have once made me feel like I couldn't go on...
But not now.
I've not only weathered the hardest downpours and survived the toughest times, I've started to learn to dance in the rain.
That doesn't mean I don't still stumble and fall, but I know now that everything that turns out bad isn't the end of the world and I can push through anything.
I'm not saying it's easy or painless, but I am saying I've learned I'm stronger than I think I am...
Especially when being strong is the only option.
No, I'm choosing not to stay down, let life get to me or letting the world get the best of me.
I'm better than that.

I'm not where I want to be yet, but I'm getting there, one step at a time.
I'm stronger, braver and wiser than I once was and instead of dwelling on what went wrong, I look for the silver lining.
I'm proud of the person that I'm becoming and I'm happier than I've ever been.
I can look in the mirror and with courage, smile and say...
"I fell apart, I survived and I kept going...
I found a way to rise from the ashes.
Now it's my time to change my world."
The next story of my life is just around the corner.
It's my favorite...
It's when I rise again,
Strong, proud and unstoppable.

She Refused to Stay Down

For everything she's been through and every failure she's overcome, she still keeps smiling and keeps fighting.
She doesn't know any other way and was never given any other choice-
Her journey often forced her to her knees and made her find her strength in ways she never thought possible.
She never had help or opportunities- she created her own chances and built her own path to the top.
Life tried to take everything from her so many times that she began to expect nothing less than hard days and steep challenges, every day.
But that's just the beautiful thing about this woman who fought to become the person she is today-
She never lamented her struggles, asked why or stayed down.
She scrapped, clawed and dug her way out of every fall, each dark place and found her way back to the light.

She'll tell you that there were many times she wanted to quit and didn't think she'd make it...
But every time, she did.
Every time, she got stronger.
Every time, she made magic out of her mayhem.
She'll never tell you that she's anything special or amazing, she doesn't think like that.
But what she will tell you with a steely facade and fierce stare is that she's a warrior.
She'll fight and struggle but she'll always come out on top.
That's just who she is now and the iron spirit she's battled to become.
So when you meet this unassuming woman with a heart of gold and an unstoppable courage, just stop and take note.
You've just crossed paths with one of the most beautiful things you'll see in this life:
A remarkable and strong woman…
And for everything she is and everything she has become,
Just appreciate her.
She's paid the price you'll never know or understand…
And you don't have to.
She did it…because that's just who she is:
She doesn't know how to quit, stay down or listen to her critics.
But what she does know is how to succeed, rise stronger and crush her goals.

I'm Not Afraid of the Fire.

I never chose this path in my life...
It chose me.
I didn't set out to be strong, I just wanted to be happy...
I ended up getting strong in the process.
The twists and the turns, the failures and falls, they all tried to bring me down.
I smiled as life tried to consume me in the fire of struggle, for it knew my warrior heart that it was forging in the flames.
I wasn't a survivor, I was a fighter.
I didn't just walk through the fire, I became it.
Truthfully, I only had two choices- rise up and rise above or plummet to rock bottom.
Strong women don't know how to quit, it's not in my genes.
I may have started this life bright eyed and innocent, but I've emerged a fiery Phoenix, able to overcome anything.

People will compliment my courageous and never-say- die attitude, because they don't know the price I've paid to become the person I am.

The hard nights crying tears, wondering why life was so hard, the challenging days when everything went wrong- they'll never know my journey to be stronger, wiser and better...

And they don't have to.

I did everything for myself, because I had dreams to chase and goals to attain- and I knew no one could get me there but me.

I've picked myself up countless times, had my heart broken too often, but I always found my way...

Eventually, I even found myself and self love along the way.

That thing called love?

I have plenty of it for myself and my people- I'm fine with my life staying that way if that's how it ends up.

I built high walls around my heart after all the bad choices that led to heartbreak, so I'm in no hurry to find true love.

If love does come calling, great, but it will have to be on my terms.

I'll never settle, sacrifice or compromise myself or my principles.

To the right one, I won't have to explain who I am…they'll just know.

So, until that person shows up, I'm going to keep flying high and loving my life...

I've paid dearly to become who I am, so I'm living every day to its fullest and chasing the things that fill my soul.
Maybe I'm not perfect, but I'm not trying to be.
I'll leave that for all the fake people following ridiculous trends to be just like everyone else.
I'm perfectly imperfect in my own beautiful unique way.
And you know what?
I'd rather be happy than perfect.
So that's just what I'll be.
My way, my style, my choices...
That's what strong women do...
And that's what I'll always be.
Anything less or different?
Well, that's for someone else.
I got this.,

I've Missed Me. Glad She's Coming Back.

I looked in the mirror and exhaled deeply.
It had taken me a long time to get to this point.
Blood, sweat and tears?
No, so much more than that.
I'd been beaten down, dragged through the mud and thrown into the fire-and that was just the start. I made the classic mistakes of giving my heart to all the wrong people in all the wrong ways and every one of those broken roads cut me a little deeper and taught me a little more-
About who I was, where I'd been and what I wanted. Sure, I hated having my heart broken time and again, but I would never change a thing about all the wrong turns I'd made.
They led me to exactly where I was meant to be-
Standing here, in front of the mirror, beginning to recognize a person I had lost a long time ago....me.

I thought by forging an identity in the people I loved and losing myself in them, I'd be happier and the love would be stronger...
And it never was.
That's not the way love works, I learned.
Real and lasting love doesn't ask a person to change into something other than who they are and I've finally started making my way back to myself, where I never should have left to begin with.
It's been a long journey full of bumps and bruises, falls and failures, but I'm finally starting to recognize the person I've been trying to find and love for way too long.
Smiling, I pulled my hair back and swiveled my hips into a fun pose.
"Girl, you've been gone way too long! Let's never do that again..."
I laughed loudly and beamed.
Sometimes, you gotta go through the hard times, try to love the wrong people and learn the difficult lessons to find your way.
It's been hard, it's been painful, it's been full of sadness...
But it's all been worth it.
I'm on my way home to better, stronger, happier version of myself, and it's a great feeling.
I'm turning my pain into power, my struggles into my strength and most of all,
My lessons into reasons...

that deep down, I needed to turn my setback into my comeback-
Wiser, stronger and with a deeper love of myself than I've ever known.
I took one last look in the mirror, grinning broadly.
"I sure did miss you, girl. Let's go remind them world why you're amazing."
And with a wink and a laugh, I kept moving forward on my journey...
This time, I'm doing it my way.

I Live Big, Don't Dare Try to Love Me Small

All my life I've been told who I should be, what I should wear or what I should look like.
I tried to do what I was told, but it just didn't take.
I was never happy fitting into their labels and boxes, so I stopped trying.
I realized that I'm unique, and I want more than to just do what everyone else is doing.
I can't and don't do anything small or halfway.
I'm not afraid to put myself out there and take risks.
Sure, I've been hurt more than my fair share, but I don't stop trying to love and be loved.
It's a risk I'm willing to take because the reward – love – is worth the price .... any price.
I know many would never agree with that, but it's my choice, and I'll take the chance without hesitation.
I've spent many sleepless nights crying myself to sleep or tossing and turning in bed, unable to rest because my mind wouldn't stop ....

But that's just part of it, and I accept that.
I refuse to stop living and stop loving because I've had my heart broken.
I learned from my mistakes, and I built higher walls around my heart, but I still give too much of myself .... that's just who I am.
I live every day to the fullest, I love with all my heart ....
And I don't plan on changing.
It's who I am – I can't love anything or anyone halfway.
So, if you think you're going to come into my life with some lackluster passion or part time friendship, think again.
I expect what I give, and I give it all.
I'm always there for my people and I always will be.
I wear my heart on my sleeve and I speak my mind .... that's just who I am.
When it comes to romance, I don't need grandiose promises or fancy dreams.
I yearn for real, authentic and genuine love: deep feeling, soul touching, heart stimulating and visceral emotional connection.
Anything less isn't enough for me.
I'm sure the world will shake its head in disapproval at the way I live and love, and they're welcome to pass judgment on me.
It doesn't mean I'll care or listen.
They don't know where I've been and don't know my reasons, so they don't have the right to think they know me .... because they don't.

So, I'm going to keep charging hard into every day with everything I have, no matter how hard the challenges may be.
I was born to become more, and that's just what I'm doing.
Big heart, big hopes, big dreams ....
And it all starts with me.
I'll keep taking the chances for amazing love and wonderful friendships because, just like I always do, I'm going to keep loving hard and living with all my heart.
It's now or never,
So, I'm choosing now.

I Will Walk Away

I have come to realize many things in this journey called life.
Most of all, that it's up to me to look after myself and my happiness.
If I can't do that, I can't expect anyone else to do that, either.
I have to go where I'm wanted and stay where I want to be...
Not try to make people like me or force myself upon anyone else.
That never turns out well.
No, I have to turn and walk away from the people, places and things that tear me down, disrespect me and make me feel badly.
If someone doesn't know my worth, it's not up to me to prove it to them.
The right people will always get me…no proving anything necessary.
They will be the ones that love me unconditionally and support me all the time, regardless of rain or shine.

I'm walking away from the rest- the toxic people, the selfish ones and the ones with agendas.
I have to do what's best for me if I'm going to be truly happy.
No more game players, users and abusers.
I'm filing my life with the unique, genuine and beautifully brave souls that enrich my life and make my heart happy.
The rest of them?
Well, they can keep doing whatever they want to do...
So long as they do it away from me.
I've got a train to happiness to catch.
Next stop: adventure.

I'm a Real Woman

I'm tired of the world trying to tell me what to be.
I'm too much of this or not enough of that...
Forget all that nonsense, I'm stepping out of the
boxes and you're not going to find a label for me.
I'm not a size, a number or just a pretty face...
I'm me, in all that ways that make me one of a kind.
I don't care what you choose to call me, but you'll
realize that I'm always down to earth and original.
Yeah, I have a lot of flaws and imperfections, but
then, who doesn't?
Oh, yes, all the fake people living pretend lives for the
attention of the people that don't care about them.
I'll pass, thanks anyways.
I'm genuine, I'm real and I'm always authentic.
I wear my emotions on my sleeves sometimes and I
have bad days, just like everyone else...
But that's the beautiful part about life.
I get to decide each and every day who I am, what I
want to be and how to look at life.
I know I can be a beautiful disaster and a complete
mess at times, but that's just part of my genuine
charm.

You'll always know where you stand with me and if you're one of my people, I'll always have your back. So, yes, maybe I don't fit the model of perfection, but then, I don't want to and I never will.

I'm beautiful just the way I am, with every flaw, scratch and curve that makes me unique.

I don't ask for permission or approval for being the amazing person that I am.

Beauty will fade but the depth of my soul and fire of my heart will always burn brightly.

I've been down some tough roads, but who hasn't? All those bumps and bruises from all the falls, failures and mistakes just made me tougher, stronger and wiser...

And I wouldn't change anything about where I've been-

I wouldn't be who I am without the fire that forged me.

So, if you want to know what a real woman looks and acts like, come hang out with me for a while.

I'm a handful, I'm beautifully broken and I'm always a little bit of a mess...

But more than that, I'm loving, I'm deep and I'm passionate about all the things that are important.

I may not be a lot of things, but what I am most is what matters:

I'm a real woman, with all my curves and flaws, living my best life and owning everything about myself with pride...

Every day, in every way, I'm always true to who I am. For me, that's exactly what makes me happy...

and I couldn't ask for anything more than that.
I'm just who I always set out to be.
Me. A real woman.
My life, my way.
Can't ask for much more than that.

I Always Find A Way to Get Back Up

If you were to ask me how I stay strong and keep going, I'll tell you that I don't know.
The storms of life roll in thunderously, trying to crash down on me and everyone in my life...
And there are those times when I'm gasping for air, but I always seem to find a way to dig deep and push through.
I've done it so much that it's not even a choice anymore, it's just part of who I am now.
Fighter.
Survivor.
Warrior.
I refuse to let the people and events of this life take me down, I'm stronger than that.
I can't deny there are days when the weight of the world crushes me and tests my limits...
But somehow, some way, every single time, I fight back and break through those walls weighing me down.
There were so many times in my past that I thought I couldn't survive, but I managed to overcome it all,

Because my spirit is strong and my courage unrelenting.
I have people depending on me and I don't have the luxury of being weak or failing.
Every day, I have countless things to do and not enough time or energy to get them all done, but I find a way.
Some people think that we are born strong because they've never seen the price we pay in blood, sweat and tears to build, grow and strengthen ourselves.
I wasn't born this way, I made myself into a strong person that would never stay down.
Life doesn't accept excuses and do overs-there's only keep going or quit.
And I'm never quitting on myself, my life or my people.
So, maybe I'm not the best at everything and some days, I look like a beautiful disaster, but I'm okay with that.
I'm doing it all on my terms, the way I want in the manner that I choose.
My life, my rules.
If you ever wonder where I am, you won't find me on the sidelines of life watching it pass me by…
No, you'll find me in the middle of the storm, dancing, fighting and doing what I do best:
Smiling and embracing the chaos.
Maybe there will be a day when I don't come out on top,
But I really doubt it.

I've got too much love, heart and spirit to ever crash and burn.
So,
Excuse me while I go out there and kick some more butt.
Oh and life,
If you're listening…Is that all you got?
I'm ready for more.
Bring it on.

I'm Proud of Who I Am Today and What It Took to Get Here

When they look at me and admire the woman that I am, I know they have no idea what it took for me to get here, and that's okay.

Though I've been in some dark places and been down some bad roads, I wouldn't change a thing about who I am or where I've been.

I've made every mistake you can think of and I've chased every bad love you can imagine, and yet, I'm still standing.

More than that, I'm thriving, growing and getting better every day.

Sure, it's hard to think back to the dark days when life brought me to my knees and I didn't know how I'd ever survive...

But I figured it out, I made a way and somehow, I ended up on the other side of the storm intact.

I'll never tell you that I didn't cry mountains of tears, get down on myself or just wonder how I would survive, because I did all those things.

It's a hard thing when you're at rock bottom and all you've got is yourself to depend on...
But that's how I forged my courage and strength- in the flames that would have tried to consume me.
I fought, I clawed and I struggled for every small victory and every little success that kept me going.
I kept climbing when I didn't have the strength and I battled to become the woman I knew that I could be- even when I couldn't find the light sometimes.
And let me tell you-
I didn't think I'd make it most days.
But that's the beauty about writing your own story....I was the one holding the pen, and I refused to give in, give up or settle for less.
I knew what I wanted and I realized what it would take, so I stopped complaining, whining and feeling sorry for myself and I turned the page to a new chapter.
I picked myself up, I fought my way back from my lowest point and I kept going, I kept fighting and started climbing.
So, yes, when I look in the mirror today, I'm very proud of the person I've become.
I earned my way here with every scratch, scar and bruise along the way.
It wasn't easy, painless or fast...
But as I stand here smiling, standing tall and proud, Through all the heartaches, the struggles and the pain, I remembered the most important thing of all:
It was worth it, every step of the way to become the woman I was always meant to be.

Sometimes Days She Has No Idea How, but Every Day It Still Gets Done

She stares in the mirror, mustering every bit of her courage and strength to take on the day.
Wiping away the beginnings of a tear, she breathes in deeply.
It's been a long week – no, make that a long year – for her.
She halfheartedly laughed.
"It's been a long forever," she said with the faint semblance of a smile.
This was one of the days she just didn't know how she was going to make it through.
She'd been up most of the night, tossing and turning …. and thinking.
It was always the endless waves of thoughts that kept her awake that made her soul weary.
Instead of waking up refreshed from the few hours of sleep she'd often get, she just woke up worried ….

About what she had to get done, the details of her tasks and whatever else her mind could jam into that space in her head.

The easier days were becoming fewer and less frequent, and the obstacles life threw at her were getting bigger and harder to overcome.

Just once, she wished, she wanted to tackle a day with all the answers.

"Or at least some of them ...."

Wistfully, she fixed her hair as she dug deep to put on the brave face that she gave the world .... You know the one, where everyone thinks you're okay, but deep down ....

"You're just hanging on by a thread."

She grimaced as her mind raced forward to what her day had in store for her.

Her closest friends knew her struggles and were there for her as much as they could be, but she knew that when it came down to it, she was the one who had to figure out a way to get it done.

People would often say they admired her resolve and strong façade, and she'd smile and make a joke about it ....

Because they didn't know.

They had no idea the fire that she walked through every day just to survive.

They had no idea what it took for her to keep going when all she wanted to do was quit.

They had no idea how she just wanted to stay in bed and hide from the world some days ....

But she couldn't.
There were people who depended on her to show up and step up every day, so that's what she did ....
without hesitation, without question.
She was so many things for so many people when she just wanted to be at peace.
Sometimes, there's a sort of weary that sleep can't fix, and that's where she was.
She needed her heart and soul to have time to recover from the wounds of her past ....
The broken hearts, the damaging pain, the forgotten promises.
She tried never to ask too much of anyone, because she'd learned the hard way that those expectations only ever led her to disappointment ....
And she'd been let down enough in her life already.
She didn't know if she could handle any more.
From the moment she stepped foot into the world until she was finally able to catch her breath late at night, there was always something to do, a task to be handled, a problem to solve ....
And it could be overwhelming.
Truthfully, she couldn't tell you how she managed to do all the things she did, only that she amazed herself sometimes.
She looked in the mirror one last time, wiping away smudges from the edges of her lipstick.
"Perfect ...."
She chuckled quietly.
"Or at least as close as I'll ever get to perfect in this life."

She smiled, exhaled and put on her brave face.
It was just one of those moments in the life of a warrior woman –
Amazing, strong and brave.
Because that's just who she is and would always be.
And every day, in every way, she always finds a way.
Just another day in the life of a hero.

Strong Women Aren't Born, We Are Forged in the Fire

I'm not going to tell you that my life has ever been easy.
There's been many times I've been on my knees, struggling to survive and fighting to keep going.
Sleepless nights, endless tears and moments of overwhelming frustration are just part of my journey.
I'd never take back where I've been nor wish for an easier road.
I know that everything happens for a reason and I've gone through the fires to build a better stronger me.
People often compliment me and remark what a strong person I am, but they'll never know the price I've paid to become the warrior that I am...
And they don't have to.
I look in the mirror every morning and realize that there is nothing that can take me down, tear me apart or stifle my success.

I may not always have it all together or know where I'm going, but I do know who I am and that no matter the storms that life throws at me, I'll always be fine. Truthfully, so many things should have broken me, ruined me and swept me under...
But survival was never just another option for me...
It was the only choice.
So, I did whatever it took, however I could, to keep my head up, keep pushing forward and I always kept smiling through it all.
Sometimes, you don't realize how strong you are until being strong is your only option...
So, those times on my knees, when I could only see the darkness, I dug deep, fought harder and refused to lose...
Myself, my dreams or my way.
It doesn't mean that there aren't days that I don't want to get out of bed, times when my smile is harder to come by and I don't know how I'm going to conquer my day...
But I always find a way, figure it out and never lose sight of the light.
I've learned that fire in your heart, passion in your spirit and magic in your soul is the ultimate recipe for strength.
I still have to remind myself to find my joy and seek happiness, but those wonderful things are always there, just waiting for me to see them.
So, at the end of the day, I'm proud of who I've become, happy with who I'm becoming and most of

all, ready to turn these claws of survival into the wings of my growth.
Watch out world,
Here I come...
And I'm about to fly higher than I ever have before.

My Strength Was Born in the Moments I was Forced to my Knees.

I'll never tell you that my journey has been easy,
but then, I own every experience along the way that has made me who I am.
The good, the bad and the ugly have built me up, broke me down and inflamed my heart like an ordinary path never could.
I've come to realize that I'm not defined by the moments that brought me to my knees, but how I rose again after falling.
I know now that I'm always going to make mistakes, have hard days and endure stormy times.
But I'll charge into those obstacles and turn them into opportunities.
My heart is alive with the fire that has forged my strength through the tough times and my soul is full with my rising from the ashes.
I'd rather burn it all down than to fail, I'm not going out like that.

I was meant for much more than to wallow in the dark and lament my struggles.
Give me the courage to always embrace the storms of today.
Give me the passion to feel alive in all that I pursue.
Give me the serenity to understand my journey and the truth of who I am.
I'll never be the baddest, the toughest or the most fierce,
But I'll never quit, I'll always be real and I'm going to embrace all my triumphs and tragedies.
This is my life and my story, and I'm choosing to live each and every day like the blessing that it is.
I've learned that it takes sadness to understand happiness, failures to comprehend victory and chaos to know peace...
And that's the wisdom I carry with me through it all... and it helps me get through the hard stuff.
Rain or shine, I'm doing it all by terms in my own way.
I'll never be perfect, and I'm good with that.
I know I'm amazing just the way that I am.
After all,
The strength of my soul was born on the backs of the moments that brought me to my knees.
It was my spirit and soul that gave me the courage to rise again.
And now, it's my wings that will help me fly higher than ever before.
Strong, alive and free

I'll Never Apologize For My Fire

I'll never apologize for how hard I love or how intense I am.
I'm passionate about everything I do and everyone I love- and that won't ever change.
I refuse to tone down, water down or filter my personality or passion for anyone who can't handle me.
I know I'm fiery, sassy and a bit spicy at times, but that's just part of my charm...
I'm not asking anyone to like me if they decide I'm not for them.
I realize that I may be an acquired taste, and I'm good with that.
There's been a lot of people who left my life that didn't always agree with who I am or what I said…and I wish them the best while respecting their choice.
I don't want anyone in my life that doesn't want to be there, all in.
I'm real, genuine and authentic in everything I say and do, so you'll know exactly where you stand with me.

I don't mince words, play fake or pretend when I don't like something or someone.
Life is too short to spend my time and energy chasing people for their affection, attention and approval when I don't need it or even want it.
I know there's people out there that will say I'm unlovable, hard to handle and opinionated, and they're right.
I speak my mind, I share my truth and I'm open and honest about what I think.
So, if anyone wants to label me, name call or write me off because they don't approve of my personality, that's their choice...
It won't change how I live my life, what I do or how I spend my time.
I'll never ask for permission to follow my heart and burn brightly for the things that matter most to me: my loved ones, my passions and of course, love, in all its forms.
Yes, I've loved the wrong people and kissed the wrong frogs, but I learned from every bad choice and I kept loving hard when there was love to be had.
I put all of my heart and soul into my love and that will never change.
It causes me to get hurt more often than I'd like, but I'll take that risk every time...
Because without putting yourself out there, you'll never know the love that could be yours...
And I'm greedy, I guess.

I want all the love from the people in my life and I'm going to enjoy every minute of it.
So, if you were waiting for an apology from me for my attitude, my passion or my words, I hate to disappoint you.
I'll admit when I'm wrong and I'll apologize when I should, but I'll never say I'm sorry for being who I am and what I love.
Being in my life is a choice, and maybe it's not for everyone, but the ones who stuck around appreciate me for all the things the world says I'm too much of: Passionate, feisty, opinionated, strong.
Maybe I'm not your cup of tea, but I know some like their coffee a bit on the strong side...
Just like me.
So, whether you like me or not, I will always be true to my word and be real.
In a world full of fake, I'd rather burn passionately and honestly for who and what I am than to be like the rest and just be a copycat.
I'm never going out like that.
If I can't do my life my way, I'm checking out.
My life, my rules, my happiness.
It's really pretty simple, if you ask me...

She's A Strong Woman with A Soft Heart and Fierce Love

She's the type of woman that men want to tame and women aspire to become.
She'll never be the sort to blend in, keep to herself or go about her life quietly...
She has too much passion, spirit and zeal for life to not make herself heard or seen.
While many shy away from her fierce nature, unable to understand her and frankly, just a little afraid of her, too.
She's that undefinable creature that inspires others just by the way she chooses to live her life.
Men are constantly enthralled by her until they realize that she's not the woman that they can control or manipulate...
Just the opposite, in fact.
She's not had the easiest life or had anything given to her, she's had to scrap for everything she has...and she appreciates everything more because of it.

It's made her strong, feisty and unstoppable....even on the days she didn't feel like she was at her best. She still kept going, climbing and fighting.

Her heart beats fiercely, for she is and always will be a warrior- rising to any challenge and always there for the people in her life.

Some would call her difficult, incorrigible or stubborn, and she just smiles and thanks them for the compliments.

Mere words will never penetrate her thick skin anymore- she's been down that road and learned those lessons the hard way.

She's heard it all and has been called everything you can imagine and it never changed anything about her other than to push her harder.

But the side of her that she keeps guarded, hidden from the world and only shared with her close friends is quite different.

Loving, generous and supportive, she's the one they can always count on to listen, love and accept without condition, every time.

She fights through life with a warrior heart and loves through life with a passionate soul.

She values both sides equally, for she knows true balance is the key to happiness.

And in the end, that's all she really wants- to be happy.

She doesn't need attention, the limelight or fancy things.

She wants the simplest that life has to offer:

Peace, happiness and love.
So, if she has to battle for those things, so be it.
But she'll never waste her time or energy on small minded people, frivolous pursuits or welcome those who can't be themselves.
But never underestimate a woman like her.
She may be many things, but you'll never find her to be a fool.
And if you happen to overlook her or count her out, well, one thing's for certain:
It'll be the last time you ever do.

Blessed Not Broken

Life had tried to tear her apart and shatter her soul, her heart and even her dreams.
But she wasn't just an ordinary woman- she was the strong woman who wouldn't be denied or stopped.
She had never really had a choice on the life path she chose- it chose her instead.
So, instead of hoping for easier days and fewer obstacles, she worked to get stronger, wiser and braver.
She'd tell you that there were many times the obstacles brought her to her knees,
But that was the most beautiful part of her ever growing strength and fierce spirit...
She refused to stay down, complain or dwell in her failures.
She dug her way out of rock bottom, she fought to keep going and no matter how hard or the challenges involved...
She always rose again.
You couldn't define her with a word, label or definition, because she was many things to many people- herself included.

Always evolving to meet the demands of her life, she would transform into whatever the situation might call for-
Loving partner, closest friend and confident , driven business person, mother, daughter...
She learned to become what she needed in every way, every day.
Sure, she had moments of weakness where she might quickly and suddenly cry, but no one ever knew it...
She'd wipe away the tears, compose herself and pick up right where she left off.
She didn't always have the answers to how she'd get everything done or how she'd find her way through a storm, but somehow, thus remarkable woman was tough, fiery and determined...
Determined to always keep going.
Determined to always keep rising.
Most of all, determined to be happy.
So, no matter how hard the day or how bad things might turn out, she'd find the silver lining in everything, somehow.
That strong woman capable of conquering the world and slaying life-she is an ever changing symbol of love, life and hope.
How do I know all of this about this amazing woman?
She is me and I'm not broken.
I'm blessed.
The rest is up to me.

But What if You Fly?

Hey you…
Yes, I'm talking to you.
You know you've been telling yourself what you can't do, how you're too old for this and too tired for that.
Well, you're wrong.
I know life has been bumpy and you've been knocked down, but lift your head, open your eyes and get up.
Don't you dare give up on your dreams and everything you've wanted.
There's so much life and love in you that you haven't even realized yet…
So it's time to stop making excuses and start making plans.
I'm not telling you that it's going to be easy, fast or painless.
I'm telling you that you can do it and that it's worth it.
Nothing worth having ever comes easily, and your dreams and desires aren't any different.
You've known what you wanted and who you've wanted to be for a long time...
Now it's time to get up, dust yourself off and start moving forward.

Stop looking over your shoulder and holding onto the painful past.
Remember the lessons but let go of the pain.
It's not doing anything but weighing you down.
You are capable of more than you know, but you're going to have to start believing in yourself- even if it's a little bit at a time.
One step after another, day after day…you'll get where you're meant to be.
Maybe it won't be where you thought you wanted to be, but you'll realize it's where you need to be.
Learn.
Love.
Live.
Grow.
Turn the page and start a new chapter.
You are worthy of great things, beautiful love and wonderful tomorrows.
Now open your eyes and start becoming the person you've always wanted to be.
You can't catch your dreams if you're standing still.
Fly, darling, fly.
You'll soon find your wings…
And you'll be glad you never gave up.
Anything is possible if you just believe.

She Kept Trying, and That Was the Bravest Thing of All

She never thought of herself as brave, she just kept doing what she had to do to survive.
In fact, most days, she felt anything but brave as the worry about what could go wrong occupied her mind.
Like everyone else, she thought of bravery as the heroic tales of fighting injustice and saving the day ....
and that wasn't her.
Far from it.
She did what she always had – she showed up, day in and day out, no matter how hard it was to get out of bed.
Regardless of how often she had cried in the shower, or how many times she wanted to scream in her car.
She was beautifully defined by those singular moments of ordinary heroism, the ones that many could muster. She kept showing up with a smile on her face even when she felt so far from happy.

In fact, just to get to this point in her life intact was a miracle unto itself – the broken roads, the failed loves, the painful disappointments ....
Everything that had happened to her would have destroyed most people ....
But then, she wasn't most people.
She was something altogether different: a brave, strong woman whose story never gave her any other choice.
It was either fail and stay down or rise up out of the ashes and keep going.
So, she did the bravest thing she knew to do:
She kept showing up, she kept trying, she kept loving.
She never lamented her broken past or her current struggles, for she was determined to build a brighter tomorrow.
She didn't know how she'd manage, but she always found a way .... that's just who she was.
Strong woman.
Proud dreamer.
Loving person.
Brave warrior.
She didn't have the answers and, most days, couldn't tell you how she'd make it through the day without crying or falling apart ....
But she did.
And she kept doing it.
Maybe she didn't realize it,
Maybe she didn't see it,
Maybe she didn't care ....

But to everyone around her for all the ways that truly matter, she was one of a kind.

Each and every day ....

She was brave, she was kind, and she was strong.

That's just who she was ....

Because she had the heart that wouldn't be denied ....

Now or ever.

In a word, she was brave.

They Doubted Me…

I looked at my bank balance and felt my heart sink.
I had less than $10 to my name and I was starving...
That night, for the first time in a long time, I went to bed hungry.
I swore to myself on that night 7 years ago that I would never forget that feeling.
So, when everyone doubted me, said I couldn't be successful or I'd never make it…
I just put my head down and did what I had to do.
I won't try to tell you that those years were easy, painless or fun.
They weren't…
In fact, they were some of the hardest times of my life.
But when your back is against the wall, you learn to either find a way or you quit.
And I was never going to be the one that quit.
Everyone doubted me.
Most wrote me off and decided I wasn't worth their time.
They left like everyone always had.

So all I had left was the person in the mirror telling me that this is not my last chapter but my first.
I scrapped, I clawed and did what I had to do.
Sometimes,
It was me against the storms of life, alone, but I held my ground.
I often thought back to that night I went hungry and remembered how it felt...every time I wanted to stay down.
And I kept getting back up, kept pushing myself and never stopped believing in me.
I was determined that if I was going to go down, I was going to do it fighting.
I didn't have anyone to pick me back up when I got knocked down or someone to call when I was hurting.
I won't tell you that I didn't have nights that seemed to last forever or days when I wanted to give up...
Cause I did. A lot.
But every day, I got a little bit stronger and a little bit wiser.
I failed, but I wasn't a failure.
I hurt, but I wasn't a victim.
I learned that you can fall to rock bottom in days but the climb back up can take years...
And I remember every day, every step, every victory and every stumble.
But I still kept getting back up, kept going.
I paid for my rise with countless tears, hard work and refusing to quit.

And when I finally got to where I wanted to be all my life, I turned around and looked back over where I'd been and how far I'd come…
And realized I wanted more.
That I was capable of more.
I learned then that they can doubt you, they can criticize you and they can write you off...
But they can't take away the success that you earn, grinding, fighting and doing what you have to do…
No one can.
Many of you have asked how I know the struggle...
This is how.
Because this?
This is my story...
It can be yours too.
Rise above and start to believe-
In you, your strength and that you're meant for more.
You got this.
Now get back up and fight for what you believe in…
YOU.

She's Once in a Lifetime

She's not the woman that will ask or beg for attention and affection, she has too much self respect to chase a man.

She's been down that road before and she knows the heartbreak from vying for the love of a man that didn't really want her...

It never turned out well when she tried to force someone's heart to love... only with her heart in pieces as she wanted something clearly not meant for her.

She realized that love must happen naturally, and no amount of coaxing, begging or asking will turn anything into real and lasting love.

She learned the lesson the hard way and she's never forgotten it.

Now, she knew what she deserved and she would no longer compete for attention, settle for less than she wanted or be okay being just an option.

They'd call her high maintenance and she'd just smile and reply,

"No, I have high standards."

She stopped trying to force the issue and instead let the suitors chase her.
Love must be natural or it will never be real…and she was prepared to be alone before she lowered her expectations.
Sooner or later, someone would come into her life and realize her worth and that she was special….
And take the time to unravel her mystery.
She was a complicated woman with complex needs, but she knew her value and would hold out for the one who saw past her eyes and touched her soul.
Until then, she'd stay strong, live free and never settle...
Most of all, she'd do it all on her own.
She knew what made her happy and was quite content to keep enjoying her life until someone came along that was good enough to make her want to share it with.
That was her choice and her journey…
She knew she was more than one in a million…
No, she was one of a kind-
And that's the only kind of love story and nav she wanted…
Unforgettable, unbelievable and of course…
Once in a lifetime,
Just like her.

Standing Alone Doesn't Mean I Am Alone. It Means I Am Strong Enough to Handle Things by Myself

I know I'm not always the easiest person to understand or get to know ....
And maybe that's just because I've been doing this life by myself for far too long ....
Maybe building high walls and keeping my guard up is part of the reason I've made it this far.
Sure, I have loving friends who are in my corner, cheering me on, and I trust them completely.
But to get to know me, to win my love, earn my trust? That's not easy for a reason.
I used to readily let people in, and they walked away, taking bits of my heart with them as they left.
When you keep getting burned, sooner or later, you stop jumping into the fire.
I've learned to stand on my own, depend on myself and fight my own battles.

Others might call it tough, strong or independent, I just call it my life.

I don't ask for approval, and I don't seek attention. I've learned to control what I can and let the rest happen as it's meant to.

I've proven to myself that I can take whatever life wants to throw at me .... time and again.

So, before you label me distant, cold or stubborn, take the time to get to know me.

Maybe I haven't had the easiest life, but I'm worth the effort.

I'm not everyone's cup of tea, but the ones who seek the truth beneath my tough exterior always seem to love and appreciate who I am.

So, forget what you think you know about an independent woman and maybe realize that you'll never know what I've had to endure to be standing in front of you today, smiling, strong and confident.

You don't know the price I've paid, the sacrifices I made or the failures that changed me.

You'll never know the roads I've traveled or the pain I've felt, but maybe if you're lucky, you'll feel the intensity of my passion ....

I love fiercely and I put it all out there – once you feel my fire, you'll realize who I am and how I love.

It's true, it's real and most of all, just like me,

It's completely unforgettable.

So, maybe I'm hard to understand, tough to get to know and even more challenging to love, but once you win my heart and affection, there's nothing I won't do for you.

And every day, in every way, I make my fiery love and intense passion completely worth the time it took to get past my walls.

Just like me …

Strong, loving and worth it all.

I am Strong, I am Loved, I am Brave, and I Will Always Be Enough

All my life, I've fought to raise my self-esteem and build myself up.
You never really forget those times as a child or a young adult when others call you names and make fun of you...
That's something that sticks with you, always in the back of your mind.
I've worked very hard to believe in myself and exude confidence, but there are those days and times when the demons of insecurity whisper to your darkest places.
Everyone tries to tell you how to look, how to dress, how to act-all the things that really don't matter in the bigger picture of things...
But I'm guilty of chasing approval from people who pass judgement on appearance for no reason other than to try to make themselves feel better...
And truthfully, it never did.

I'm done with trying to seek the favor of those for things I don't care about.
I want to be known for the beautiful qualities I have, not how pretty I am...
There's so much more to me than what I'm wearing or my external beauty.
Show me the way to the people that praise depth, love passion and enjoy character...
I'm walking away from all those fake people who concern themselves with unimportant details in a world obsessed with fake perfection.
I'm imperfect, I'm flawed and I'm always going to have bad days-that's just life.
But as I look in the mirror, I know that those things don't define me, they motivate me to try harder.
My scars tell the story of where I've been and my heart sings the melody of where I'm going.
I have times of insecurity and indecision, but we all do.
Taking a deep breath, I close my eyes and exhale slowly.
Opening my eyes, I see the woman staring back at me and I'm starting to see more than all the bad stuff I used to fixate on.
It's not easy as my eyes try to drift to my imperfections and flaws, but I know now I'm more than that.
I done focusing on the things that don't matter and I'm going to begin believing in the things that do.

I'm strong because I've survived the fire and risen again.
I'm brave because I dug deeply and found the courage to start believing and loving myself in the way I should have.
I'm loved by the people in my life who appreciate me for all of my beautiful disaster and glorious mess that makes me special...
And I'm now learning to put myself and my needs first....including love.
As a smile begins to curl the corners of my mouth, I start to remember the magic that has made me amazing all along.
I'm more than enough...
and I always will be.
This year, I'm showing myself and the world just how high I can fly.
No matter what happens or how hard life can get...
There's nothing stopping me from flying higher than I ever have before.

A Strong Woman May Break Down a nd Cry, But She Will Always Rise Again .

When you meet her, you'll be amazed at her courage to attack her days and her seemingly unbreakable strength.

She a woman unlike any other- she's very real with a heart of gold and an unstoppable spirit.

But what you don't see are the moments when this strong and beautiful woman steals away from life, determined to find some much needed time to recollect herself.

Underneath the fierce armor of a facade she projects is a sensitive and caring soul that gets beaten down and hurt at times…

But she's also proud and resilient, so she tucks away the hurt and weariness until she can make the time to patch her emotional holes and rekindle her spark.

She'll never be without feelings, for she follows her heart and listens to her soul…

She's a deeply empathic person who is always connected to the people around her-
Even if it often drains her and makes her weary...
So, whatever she does to rebuild her energy, she finds moments here and there to reclaim her fighting spirit....sometimes, tears momentarily stain her face as she releases her pent up frustrations...
In the shower, in the car, in the bathroom at work...
Wherever she can scrounge up the time for herself, she holds on to those quiet times tightly.
Those are instants of respite that allow her to keep going, stay strong and be a fighter.
She's not weak or needy, she's human.
She's strong when she has to be, and in her life, that's all the time...
So, when you see her, you'll never know the tears she sheds behind closed doors and the emotional wounds she patches up quietly...
For she's a strong woman,
And she'll always be a warrior with heart.
She'll tackle any obstacle, love her people hard and live each day to its fullest...
And she'll do it all with a smile on her face.

You'll Always See the Fire in Her Eyes

he's not the one who easily shares herself with the world, she's mastered the art of disguising her deepest emotions behind a steely facade.
Not because she's scared to show the world who she really is, but because she chooses to share her authentic truth with the ones who truly love and appreciate her.
Her fierce persona isn't for the weak of heart or lackluster souls out there, so she gives the world only what it needs to see.
The bits and pieces of her that are normal are what she projects to everyone else- she realized a long time ago that she wasn't for everyone...
And she's fine with that, so she keeps the special parts for the people who get her.
She lives her life fully, loses herself in the beautiful moments of each day, but make no mistake about it-
She's paid dearly to get where she is...

Some might even say she's been to hell and back.
She just calls it life.
She doesn't complain, worry or ask for help to tackle the challenges that have always come her way…
She does what she does best:
Fight harder, keep going and find a way.
Maybe it's not always easy,
Maybe there's days she wants to quit,
And maybe she just wants to rest…
She chooses her moments, finds her ways to recharge and keeps evolving, fighting and growing.
She's not just any women, she's a warrior that refuses to accept defeat-
Whether it's in her personal life, career or just the daily tasks,
She's always strong, resilient and able to overcome anything.
So, when you see her heavenly smile greeting you on the street, realize that you may never know the gorgeous depths that lie beyond her facade,
But with a single glimpse, you'll never mistake the roaring fire in her eyes...
Beautiful, fierce and strong,
Just like her.

She has a Heart of Gold in Search of Peace and Love

She made the choice a long time ago to never surrender to the problems and challenges that tried to bring her down.
She never set out to become strong, tough or brave, her story never gave her another option.
She's always done whatever it takes to make it where she's trying to go, but she's never sold her soul or sacrificed her values to reach her goals.
She's not perfect, and she gave up trying to be a long time ago.
She's made her fair share of mistakes, wrong turns and bad love choices, but that never dissuaded her from pressing forward.
She never asked "why me," she just found a way through the struggles, every time.
She's more than just a simple woman, though you may not know that at first glance.
She's a warrior spirit, with the soul of a dreamer and the heart of a lover...

More than anything, she's been searching for peace and love since the very beginning.
She's always been that person that loves with all her heart-
Herself, her people, her life....and perhaps, one day, her "forever person," when he shows up.
She's never questioned the timing of life; she's learned to do the hardest thing of all:
Trust.
Herself, her heart, life's timing, all the things that she should have stopped believing in so long ago, but never did.
She's had her heart broken into a million pieces and she's always been the one to pick up the pieces and put herself back together again...
Each time better and stronger than before.
She's a complex person with simple needs and she's never abandoned her desire to be happy in the things that matter.
She's more than a survivor- though, some days, she felt like that was all she was doing.
Most importantly, she's always kept her fire burning and kept her light shining brightly in her eyes-always believing in herself throughout it all.
Maybe one day she'll rest and take some time for herself....but that time isn't now.
She still has much to do and an entire future full of possibilities....
Falling in love with being alive every day.
Strong, beautiful and free.

One day,
She'll be in love with herself and her life, finally at peace and content, perhaps, even more...
And she can't wait to finally be happy and rest-
She's earned all of that and more....a long time ago.

It's My Time to Fly

People often come up to me and express their admiration for my strength and ask me how I do it.
I'll just shrug and tell them I don't know.
If I told them why I am the way that I am, they wouldn't understand, and I don't expect them to.
My story isn't a simple one of victory, it's so much more than that.
Every scar, every scratch, every flaw... they are a reminder of who I am and where I've been.
It's been a long, hard road full of defeats and tears...sleepless nights and times at my wits end.
There were so many times I didn't know how I would make it through the day, much less build a future and chase dreams...
No, those were for the people who had it figured out and I wasn't one of those.
I was the fly by the seat of my pants and make it work somehow kind of person...
It wasn't usually pretty, sometimes ugly, in fact, but I always ended up where I needed to be- even if it wasn't where I set out to go.

Life has a way of giving us what we need, not what we think we want- It's been a hard lesson, but one that I had to learn if I was ever going to evolve into the person I was meant to be.

Behind every heartbreak came a lesson and through each disappointment, I learned a little more about myself.

I realized my value and what I wouldn't take any more, especially in love.

Day by day, step by step, I grew a little more, forged a stronger will and kept building my courage.

It wasn't easy every time I got knocked down, but I was determined to never stay down or accept defeat.

So, when people admire me for my journey that they'll never know, I just smile and thank them for their compliment.

They'll never know what I overcame and how I forged my strength in the fires of failure,

and that's okay, they don't have to.

It's my story and I'm the hero.

I'm stronger, wiser and happier than I've ever been before, and I'm only going to get better...

as Is my life.

I know that I'm right where I'm meant to be doing exactly what I'm supposed to be doing.

I'll just keep climbing to the top, because that's just who I am.

I'm no longer just a survivor, I'm much more than that. I'm a warrior...

And I can and will do anything so long as I believe-

starting now, starting to believe in myself.
This is my story and this is my time.
Finally, I know something I never did before
I got this and I always will.
It's my time to fly and shine.

She's Strong and That's Just Who She Is.

She's a strong woman with a intense personality…and she makes no apologies for who and what she is.
All the men gush about how amazing she is, how they admire her strength and pursue her with relentless intent…
But the thing is, most of them just like the idea of her- the real and authentic woman that she is will always be too much for most of those chasing her…
They don't understand the kind of woman she truly is and what it takes to love a person like her.
Her needs and desires are simple enough- love and be loved, respect and loyalty…
Ideals that are much more than just words to her….they are part of her values.
She's not one to be taken lightly or dismissed easily, for she goes after what she wants and doesn't know what defeat is.

The weaker men fancy themselves to be something other than what they truly are- for it takes a strong man to run with this lioness...

And none of them fit that bill, though they don't seem to realize it.

She's not content with those of lackluster character or ordinary passion.

She needs more- no, she craves the one who can ignite her heart and connect with her soul...

And that's no easy task given the wall she has built around her inner depths to protect herself.

Many have tried and all have failed, because in her world, she's not going to settle, wait or be an option.

She demands the best of those who stay in her life, just as she gives...

All of her heart, every bit of her soul and loyalty that knows no end.

The ones that come along seeking temporary satisfaction and superficial desire don't ever get a chance ...she knows the look and feel of a coyote in wolf's clothing.

She carries herself with dignity, class and courage and expects the same from any that would attempt to love her.

They'll push her away, saying she's overbearing, too demanding or too much...

And yes, she'll gladly tell anyone that's she's too much for those who aren't strong enough to run with her.

She'll never be happy with just anyone, because she doesn't actually need anyone.

She loves herself completely and values her time and independence...

So, if someone wants to step up and vie for her affection, they'd better be prepared to be patient, true and genuine, for her world isn't one that tolerates fake or insincere.

She's been down that road too many times before and burned that bridge so that she'd never go back.

She's always trusted the way things worked- and if love was meant for her, it would show up when the time is right, not a minute before.

So, she made sure that the weaker men with false intentions could save their time, energy and shallow requests...

She wasn't stopping for a distraction that would never earn her heart.

Maybe she was tough, she was definitely strong, but she would always be one of a kind...

And until someone came to change her mind, she'd keep living her best life.

Strong, beautiful and free.

You are Enough, and You Are Not Alone

I'll never tell you that I've always been strong and able to do what I put my mind to.
No, just the opposite, in fact.
I've spent too many sleepless nights wondering how I was going to survive the hard times in my life.
I would feel sorry for myself for what I was going through and ask "why me?"
The question I should have been asking was "why not me?"
Because for every challenge that I thought might destroy me, each battle that threatened to pull me under...
There was a light inside me that wouldn't let me quit.
In fact, I never realized that or understood how I was always able to keep showing up, keep going and keep rising above.
I won't tell you it was easy, painless or fast,
But in every storm, I found meaning.

Behind each obstacle, I found strength.
So, when I was wishing my life would be easier ,
I should have been grateful for the courage and strength that I built through the struggles.
I used all the negativity of other people who never gave me a chance as my fuel to dig deep and come back fighting.
I found my why.
Why I was determined to succeed.
Why I wanted more.
Why I wouldn't rest until I climbed the mountain in front of me.
So, when I wake up in the morning and stare in the mirror, I don't see the tired, frustrated and weary person that I once was.
No, I see something very different.
A brave soul with a hopeful heart, indomitable spirit and a will to overcome that never quits.
So, to all the people who said that I'd never make it, amount to anything or being to succeed,
Thank you.
Your words became the fuel for my battles and power for my spirit.
Without you, I'd never have found myself.
And you know what?
I got this…
And I always will.

Don't Worry About Being Beautiful, Be Authentic

I used to spend my days trying to be what I thought would make everyone else happy and help me fit in.
Truth is, nothing of that ever made me happy or helped me feel good about myself.
They told me to be pretty, be this or be that.
I realized then they didn't care who or what I was, they just wanted me to help them feel better about themselves by making me fit into their little boxes and labels ....
It made them feel in control, and they thought it helped them understand me ....
But that wasn't my truth.
And I'm done playing by their rules. I'm done trying to become something I was never meant to be.
I don't care about being labeled, understood or fitting in.
What matters to me is being true to myself, and I'll never be able to do that chasing their dreams.

Beautiful? Pretty? Trendy?

Those are words that don't matter to me because they're not real.

What's real is who I am and the things about me that are awesome.

Intelligent, witty, authentic, fun .... the list goes on and on, because I'm a unique person blessed with original qualities.

Please don't try to describe me with a generic word meant to box me in or make me seem like everyone else ....

Because I'm far from it.

Call me quirky, outrageous and all those fun words that mean I make some people uncomfortable.

I can't help but laugh at the thought of it.

I know they don't understand why I choose to be the way that I am, and they don't have to.

I like who I am, and I like my life ....

From my weird friends – who I adore for their weirdness – to the love I share to the adventures I chase ....

It's all a reflection of me, and I like who I'm becoming.

Maybe I won't win an award for being "the best of everyone just like me," but I'll be happy, original and one of a kind.

Having a content soul and full heart matters much more to me than impressing people I don't care about in ways that don't matter for attention I don't want.

So, save the simple, superficial words to describe someone else – maybe someone who thinks those words are wonderful.

I'll stick to being who I am and wholly indescribable. Because at the end of the day, those words can never even get close to the awesomeness that is me.

Even The Strong Need Rest

I don't know how to be any other way than the strong, independent person that I am.
I've braved the struggles of my life for so long, it's just become ingrained in my spirit that I can do anything, overcome everything.
I've been battling the fires that tried to consume me for as long as I can remember.
But there are those days when the world just comes crashing down all around me and I'm fighting just to keep my head above water.
No matter how I try to say that I'm always fine, I still get tired...
And I truly need the type of rest that sleep alone can't cure.
My body gets tired and my soul becomes weary...
And I just need some peace and tranquility.
I don't need much-
Give me any amount of time- five minutes, half an hour....and I'll enjoy every fleeting moment of that stolen time to recharge my fire.

If you want to know my secret of how I get everything done and conquer the world without batting an eye, that's it.

Seeking solace in the quiet times that I scoop up during my days to rest my soul.

I treasure those moments of solitude, for that is what keeps me going...

That and the love of my people, my zest for life and my "never say die" attitude.

I always want to be able to look back over my life, everything I've accomplished, the people I've loved and the happiness that I've created and know that I gave it everything I had.

I left no person unloved, no challenge unconquered and no dream unrealized.

After all, when it's all said and done,

They may forget what I've said or done, but they'll never forget how I made them feel.

You're Right, I'm A Lot.

All my life, I've heard a lot of the same things...
I'm a handful, I'm too much, I'm a lot to take in.
Well, all I can say to that is good!
If I'm too strong for most people's taste, then I'm doing something right, I think.
I'm not trying to be memorable, stand out or be different...
I'm just unique.
People that shine brighter catch the eyes of others because of who they are, not because they're trying to be the center of attention.
Weaker men would try to tell me to tone it down, scale it back or be a little less me.
So, I did what anyone should do when I heard that...
I turned up "me" even more.
If they can't handle me at my normal level of amazing, what makes them think they can handle me at any level?
They can't, they won't and I don't really care.

I've never sought approval to be who I am or asked anyone's permission for my personality.
I just am who I am without apology or regret.
Sure, I may stick my foot in my mouth by saying the wrong things sometimes and I may not be the quietest one around, but you'll always know where you stand with me and what I think, however that plays out.
There's a lot of people pretending to be a lot of things to impress others who really don't care in ways that aren't important.
What counts is what I think of myself and the love I have for myself and my people.
I'm always real, authentic and genuine…and not everyone likes that.
Oh well, that's their loss.
Asking me to tone it down is like asking the sun to stop shining,
So I think I'll keep doing what I do best and be the best version of me that I can be.
It may not always be pretty, it may not always be perfectly put together, but at least I'll always be true to myself.
So, to all those people who told me I'm "too much" or "a lot", you're right-
I love too much, I trust too much, I care too much and I love too much….if that's even possible.
No, I'm a lot of all the things that matter- a lot of depth, a lot of fun, loving and loyal...
And nothing or no one will ever change that.

I'm not asking for your permission to fly, I'm just going to keep spreading my wings and soaring like I was always meant to do.

Maybe one day, they'll stop worrying what I'm too much of and start appreciating me for the amazing person I am.

Until then, I'll keep flying high, loving hard and losing myself in the moments of my life.

Catch me if you can.

My Passions Burn Brighter Than My Fears

I never thought of myself as strong, brave or anything like that until I realized one day I had been forced down that road a long time ago.
I was never given a choice on who and what to become- I did what I had to do to survive.
Sometimes, you don't think about the path you choose, because there's no other option.
That's just how I became the person I am today- strong, independent and fiery.
Sure, I was afraid a lot of days and there was more than one time I quickly erupted into emotions and cried in the shower...
But I always kept going.
I never gave up and I fought through every challenge and storm with passionate fury.
But that's the thing about me:
My passion- for my life, for my people, for my dreams- will always burn so much brighter than any fears that might pop up.

I don't always know how I get everything done and how I make it through some hard days, but that's just who I am now.

I'm a warrior with a heart of gold and a spirit forged in the fire of struggle.

I love hard when I choose to and I put all of my heart and soul into everything I do and everyone I love.

There's no such as half way or too much in my book...

I live and love with the force of a thousand fires...

And no matter what happens every day, you'll always see me with a smile on my face and determination in my walk.

This is my life, my way and I'm stronger than I've ever been before.

I've got this and I always will.

The Strong Turn the Pain into Power

She hasn't had the easiest life- in fact, it has often brought her to her knees.

While the people she meets would marvel at her strength, they don't know the struggles she's endured to become the woman she is today.

Yes, she's found a way to dig deep and rise above the fire that once threatened to tear her apart.

She still cries in the shower sometimes and fights to keep it together....but she knows what it takes now to keep moving forward.

There's still days that she battles just to keep a smile on her face, but she's become used to that- she's a fighter.

She's walked through the fire, risen from the ashes and did what she had to do to survive the hard times...

And she doesn't regret any of it.

She learned from the toughest challenges what it takes to do more than simply survive....she wants to thrive and be happy, most of all.

She is done living day to day and heartbreak to heartache.
She's determined to thrive, rise above and find her wings again.
She's not a princess, a damsel in distress or a starry eyed girl in search of love.
She's turned her pain into power and transformed herself into a queen...
Never settling, accepting no excuses and no longer allowing anyone to mistreat or disrespect her.
She'll admit that she doesn't have all the answers and she doesn't always know what her days will bring....and she's more than okay with that.
She's gritty, courageous and full of zeal.
Maybe she falls and stumbles, perhaps she takes some wrong turns and makes some bad decisions.
She owns her mistakes and appreciates life in the small moments of beauty that she sees.
To her, strong is the new pretty and she's not out to impress or win anyone's approval.
She's happy living her best life and spreading sparkle, love and sassy wherever she goes.
Oh, and one more thing...
When they try to call her "princess", "hot", or "sweetheart," she'll just smile at them and remind them in the most charming way she knows how...
"I think you're mispronouncing queen, darling."
And with a smile and a wink, they realize that she's one of a kind...
Queens aren't born, they're made.
With her crown forged in the fire, she was made to be great.

I Am Not What Happened to Me, I Am What I Choose to Become

I fought for so long to simply survive my life, trying to get by day to day.
I'd get up most days wondering how I'd make it, mustering up my courage and strength to keep going.
I got knocked down, dragged around and left to fail, time and again.
The world didn't give me a chance and, frankly, I don't know that I did, either.
But when you're stuck at the bottom and trying not to suffocate, you make a choice:
Either give up and accept failure or you dig deep, find something brave in yourself and rise up again.
Truth is, my life and my story never gave me a choice ....
There were too many people and there was too much to lose to just give up ....
So, I did the only thing I knew to do.

I braved the flames of my struggles, and they lit my soul on fire.
You learn a lot about yourself when you're alone at rock bottom, fighting for survival, trying to find the strength to keep going.
I did.
I chose not to be defined by what happened to me or by where I've been.
I forgave the people along the way that hurt me, and I started to let go of the pain that I had let shackle me
....
That's not who I am.
For too long, I had let past pain dictate my life.
Not anymore.
I'm accepting responsibility for the choices I've made and where I've been.
I'm making peace with my past so that I can build a better future, piece by piece.
It's not easy – I still have days when the memories haunt me, and the pain comes back to visit.
But I do what I have to do, and I push through those times.
I still have days when I cry in the shower, and I have times where just getting out of bed takes everything I have.
Maybe that's just part of the journey.
My days won't all be great, and they can't all be bad, I get that now.
I find the small victories in the hard days, and I appreciate the good times.

But most of all, I never forget where I've been and the people who helped me forge my strength along the way.

I'm not a victim, a survivor or broken.

I'm a fighter, I'm a warrior, and I'm strong.

Because I choose to be.

Maybe it's not always pretty or easy, but I'm going to own my experiences and keep striving to be a better person, every day in every way.

I look back and wonder how I kept going sometimes, but then I realize I had to go through the hardships to get stronger, wiser and better.

Because of everything, I can smile now and know, no matter what:

I got this.

She is Strong and Chooses to Stay Positive

She hears the whispers behind her back...mindless talk from people that don't really know her.
She sees all of the negativity from others around her but continues on her path.
She's heard it all before, even tried to stop the gossip and talk behind her back...
To no avail.
They've long since made up their minds about her and she's learned that nothing she can say or do will change their ignorant opinions about her.
Let them think what they will- it doesn't change anything about her days and it doesn't even matter in the long run.
She knows who she is and what she can do, even knows where she is headed.
Those small minded people won't be where she's going, for happiness and success aren't populated with their like.

They don't know what to make of her and they certainly can't tame her or keep up, so they do the only thing they know to do:
They talk.
She hears their chatter and simply smiles, knowingly.
She's better than to lower herself and waste her time.
She has dreams to catch and passions to pursue and they'll never be part of those plans.
She knows what she has to do and how-so, she walks past those people.
Her life, her loves and her future are too important than to spend energy and time on things and people that don't matter.
She's fierce, she's strong and she knows what she wants.
They all showed her who she never wanted to be, so she chose the other path.
And as she climbs higher, dreams bigger and loves harder...
She's the diamond who will keep shining brighter with more pressure...
Strong, proud and free,
She can do anything she wants,
Starting with simply being happy. And sometimes, changes are so gradual that you can't even really see them at first.
So, she didn't think about it as she kept pushing forward and fighting for her happiness.
And eventually the hard days began to grow a little easier and the things that used to weigh her down began to feel a little lighter.

Her strength grew and so did her joy.
She hadn't set out to be strong, but she had much more to do in her life and she would need every iota of strength, bravery and courage to persevere.
Even through the times that brought her to her knees.
Even through the times that broke her.
But the bitter sweetly beautiful thing that also happened?
She got up, dusted herself off and started to put herself back together again each and every time.
If not for the hard roads she'd traveled, she'd never have had what she needed to fight through the trials of her life and keep going.
Her struggles had transformed her into a strong and independent woman.
Looking back, she'd never change where she'd been, because she knew that's what it took to make her the person she became.
On the way to an extraordinary life, she became all the things she never thought she could ....
A strong woman.
A warrior.
A believer ....
Most of all, a Phoenix rising ....
And her time was now.
Through the ashes and fires that had once consumed her,
She finally became strong enough to choose ....
To become whoever she wanted to be.

She Finds A Way To Always Get it Done

She never set out to become strong, independent or resilient, but life had other plans.
She didn't choose the path her life took- it chose her...
So she did what she had to do, grew stronger when she needed to and learned how to fight back, rise above and keep going...
Even when she felt like quitting so many times.
That's not who she is or will ever be, though.
She doesn't know how to stay down, accept defeat or be okay with giving up.
Truth is, she never saw half of what happened coming and she definitely had no idea how to make it through...
But she figured it out-
She always has.
It might not always be graceful, well planned or executed flawlessly...but she gets it done.

She's not always had the strength or fortitude to push through and there were so many times she thought life would pull her under, but somehow, she would fight through.

The storms she has survived have made her appreciate the rainbows after the rain...

And she's thankful for the moments that have turned into memories, people that turned into friends and the setbacks that turned into comebacks.

There will always be hard days, formidable challenges and stormy times...

But she's learned to never let it overwhelm her or make her question herself.

She'll find the answers, figure out the path forward and dig deeply to find her strength- she always has.

She's more than a survivor, she's a warrior with a heart of gold and an iron will.

For her, this life wasn't ever a choice-

It's who she was meant to be.

And as surely as tomorrow will rise, the first rays of sunrise will find her doing what she does best...

Living purposefully and loving passionately.

She's got this,

And she always will...

Because she is me...

And I'm a strong woman,

And that's what strong women do.

Overcome, fly high and shine brightly.

She Became Unstoppable

She didn't choose the hard path in life, it chose her.
She was never given another option but to fight for everything and everyone she ever loved.
She learned the hard way that life can be a merciless master if you let it...
But she chose never to be a victim, complain or wallow in her defeats and setbacks.
There were always days when she didn't want to get out of bed, cry momentarily in the car or the shower, but she'd always wipe the tears away and appear unblemished and unshaken to the world.
That was her gift, in fact...
To be brave on the outside when she was sometimes falling apart on the inside.
But the day that changed it all was when she realized how to use the pain to transform her life.
She learned how to turn the pain into power...
Power to stand up and be heard.
Power to set boundaries.
Power to keep rising again after she broke.

That was the day her life began to change and she never looked back.

She harnessed the passion and determination born of countless struggles and intense heartache.

She stopped looking back in regret and started looking forward with a fire roaring behind her eyes.

She decided she would no longer be denied the things in life she wanted:

She would chase, battle and struggle for what she wanted and deserved...

And she didn't need any help or motivation...

She just did what she had to do, each and every day.

She knew she'd fall, she'd still hurt and there would be setbacks.

But more than that, there would be her unwavering determination to keep getting up, keep rising again and keep getting stronger every time.

She didn't have the answers to where her life would lead her or why things happened, but she did know one thing:

She was unstoppable...

and she would always rise again.

Not Everyone Can Be Strong All The Time

I've known all my life I wasn't the easiest person to love, but then, I never wanted to be.
I knew it would take a special person to appreciate my uniqueness and qualities, so I never lowered my standards to accommodate lesser love…
I'm just not built that way.
When I love, I do so with all my heart and soul, I don't do anything halfway and that's what I expect in return.
I have a lot of love to give and I'm passionate in everything I pursue.
I learned a long time ago that there's many who say they love a strong woman…until they realize that maybe they can't handle all of me.
That's okay, I'm never going to settle, compromise or accept less than I deserve.
I've battled, struggled and fought too hard to become the person I am to just give it away to give my heart to someone that won't appreciate it.

They'll say I'm too much- too much opinion, too much intensity, too much attitude...
But the truth is, I'm just too much for them.
I'm not ever going to be everyone's favorite flavor and I don't see eye to eye with all that I meet...
But the ones that get me- truly get me- we just click...
And it's one of the most beautiful feelings I know.
Those are my people and the ones I'll always cherish- my tribe.
In the meantime, I'll just keep doing what I do best- living my life fully and staying strong.
I know that somewhere, someone will come along that will love me just as I am.
Until then, I'll be flying high and being happy.
I'll never go wrong with loving myself and chasing my dreams...
One day at a time.

My Fiery Heart Will Never Be Tamed

Call me difficult, challenging or stubborn....whatever you'd like, it doesn't matter to me- I've heard it all before from weaker people that couldn't handle me... But you'll find that if you can muster the courage to run with me, you'll always find the yearning burning deep inside you to call me yours.
I'm not the one you bring home to momma or the one who will ever play house, so if that's what you need, I'm sure you can find plenty of gals up to that task.
No, I'm the incorrigible feisty fiery one- the woman who you don't want to fall for, but just can't help it.
I have a passion on fire in my heart that draws you in…it makes you crave the burn.
You'll tell yourself you don't need me, don't want me, that I'm a waste of your time...
And maybe you'll even believe that for a time.
But we both know that I'm the unquenchable thirst for life, love and chaotic desire that you can't turn away from.

I'm not looking to someone to settle down with, I need the one who hears the call of the wild in my soul and hungers to answer it with me.

Maybe I'm a little reckless, perhaps even a bit of a mess, but I'm real, I'm genuine and you'll always know where you stand with me.

But if you choose to chase my affection, don't bring any lackluster feelings or lukewarm passion...

I need just the opposite- too much of everything that'll burn you alive.

Too much passion.

Too much intensity.

Too much love.

If you're not willing to take the plunge with me and push the boundaries of life and love, then you may want to find someone a little more...

Bland.

Cause I'm not her and I won't ever be the one okay with anything halfway.

If you think you're strong enough to run with me, brave enough to love my fierce heart and wild enough to see it through,

Then let's go lose ourselves under the stars and chase dreams of shadows that once were.

Tonight, in these moments, we can love and live forever...

That is, if you can keep up.

A Woman Determined to Rise

She didn't know she ended up at rock bottom, cast aside, left for dead and forgotten.
It hurt worse than anything she'd ever known – and she'd been through some hard times.
All her life, she was kicked around, pushed aside, disrespected and disregarded.
When you get treated so badly and told you're worthless for so long, you start to believe it.
But this last man, someone who promised her that he'd be there forever, crushed her soul with his hateful words.
He swept her away with delusions of grandeur and then cast her aside just as quickly ....
It's one thing to break someone's heart, it's quite another to tread on it ruthlessly.
He left her crying and feeling less than worthless as he moved on effortlessly.

One look at her would tell you that she was a broken woman – she had nothing left, her heart and soul pulverized once again by lies disguised as promises. But as she was laying there, sobbing and heartbroken, something snapped.

She didn't know what happened or what changed, but she felt something welling inside that she had never felt.

A small spark of courage whispered to her in her darkness.

"Get up .... rise again .... you're better than this."

Truthfully, she couldn't really tell you what happened next, but she dried her eyes, pulled her hair back and glared fiercely into the mirror.

She exhaled forcibly and a gleam slowly appeared in her eye.

Her voice cracked as she spoke words she'd never forget.

"Never again."

Never again would she allow anyone to disrespect and mistreat her.

Never again would she settle for less than she deserved.

Never again would she stay down.

She knew it would be the hardest thing she'd ever done .... but then, after you've got nothing to lose, there's nowhere to go but up.

She pulled herself up and made a promise to herself that she intended to keep.

"No matter how hard, how long or how painful this may be, I'm going to rise from the ashes and become the fire that once burned me down."

No more excuses and no more apologies.

Just her and a fierce determination to fight, claw and battle her way back.

She was done asking for permission and determined to forget the pity party.

She didn't know where she was going or how she'd get there, but anywhere was better than where she was ....

Day by day and step by step, she'd forge a new path out of the pain and into the light ....

Afterall, there is no force equal to the strength of a woman determined to rise.

She Will Rise , Always…

She's finally hit the point where she's done with it all.
She's done with people letting her down, trying to disrespect her and hurt her.
No more.
She has been beaten down and hit rock bottom, but she's not staying there.
She's been lost for too long and it's her time now.
She's rising up from the ashes with the courage of a thousand warriors and the roar of a million lions.
No longer will she accept failure, mistakes and struggle.
She's been trapped in the fires of life for too long and she's choosing to become more.
She's the Phoenix that cannot be stopped and she will rise up above those that would see her fail.
Bruises, dents and scratches won't dissuade her from pushing forward and rising up.
Her veins are coursing with the fiery passion that fills her spirit and she won't be denied.
She's been denied, put off and disregarded for far too long.

She's turning the page, setting her world ablaze and taking back her life.

Pain from her past is the fuel for her ascent and she's on fire with an undeniable hunger to rise above, to succeed, to start realizing her dreams.

Those words that used to define her …"can't", "won't", "shouldn't"…those are forgotten, never to be uttered again.

The world has never seen a creature like her, with an indomitable drive to find her wings and fly higher than she ever knew she could.

She's leaving behind the haters, the jealous, the disbelievers and anyone else that won't stand by her side as she fights her way to the top.

She knows what she deserves and she's not settling for anything less than what she wants.

She's waited her entire life for this one chance to become what she was always meant to be.

No more second guessing, hesitation or questions.

She's doing what she has to do to push through and fight for her dreams.

It won't be easy- her life never has been….but this time, she won't be denied.

She's more than a warrior, a strong woman or a lioness,

She is a Phoenix rising,

And her time is now.

She's Not Distant, She Just Refuses to Be Disrespected

She's not cold or distant, she's anything but everything they would have you believe.
No, she doesn't let anyone take advantage of her and she won't let just anyone past her walls....but she has her reasons.
Everything that she is and everything that she has learned has come from a life of struggle and heartache... even the battles she's fought to become who she wanted to be.
She's made bad decisions and she's chosen the wrong people to love, but it never kept her from holding her head high and still believing in love.
People that don't try to understand her or see past her steely resolve will always misinterpret her facade as hostile or bitter, but they couldn't be more wrong.
She's had to learn how to protect her heart from all the people that she used to let hurt her.

She's had to fight for her happiness every step of the way, so she's learned to appreciate the joy in all the moments of life- both big and small.
She's had to claw, battle and dig deep to make it through some of her days...
But she's still standing.
More than that, she's got a smile on her face and fire in her heart.
Life can't bring her down- it already tried that and failed.
She's been through hell and back, that's how she became the fire that sparks her spirit.
She's not easy to love or quick to know, but she's worth the effort- any effort- because a woman like her doesn't come around often.
Those who seek to love her must have patience, truth and authenticity in their actions or she'll walk away.
She's been lied to, hurt and broken so many times that she's lost count...
But that's what made her strong, that's what forged her strong will.
She's learned her worth the hard way after being put down, mistreated and taken for granted- she vowed long ago to never let anyone treat her that way again.
People think because of her smile and gentle laugh that she's just like everyone else...
And they're so very wrong.
She's the fire you don't forget and the diamond that sparkles after all the struggles.

She'll never settle, be disrespected or be treated as just another option.
Rain or shine, bad days or good, she's always true to her word and real in her actions.
She doesn't need a partner, charity or pity...
She knows who she is and what she wants...
Love- for herself, for her people and for the things that matter.
So, when you meet her, just accept her as she is and love her how you can...
To know her, love her and be a part of her life is to appreciate someone very special.
After all, the strongest people can often have the deepest love of all...
Cherish that love, for if she chooses to share that side of her with you,
That's the most beautiful gift of all:
Her heart.
Protect it and you'll always be glad you did.

I Can Overcome Anything

I'll never tell you it was easy getting knocked down and hurt so many times in my life.
The hard days when I felt like I wouldn't make it…everyone I met let me down and it seemed like every decision I made just hurt me-
Those are the scars that I think about every day…
But that pain, failure and anguish that tried to tear me apart?
It didn't…
It just made me stronger, wiser and braver.
I think often about those scars -reminders of darker days, harder times and broken hearts….and I promise myself every day to never stay down, never quit and to never stop believing in myself.
I won't tell you it gets any easier, because no matter how much pain I've endured, how many times I've clawed my way out of rock bottom…
It's still gut wrenching and hard every time.
I may now finally have the strength and motivation to push through the storms and battle my way past the

pain, but it's been an uphill battle every step of the way.
I used to wish for easier days and more sunshine…
But now I know that the journey is just part of my preparation for bigger and better things…
And I'm not stopping until I reach the top.
I look in the mirror every day and stare at myself and remember those deepest of cuts…
And I promise myself each time that every cut, scrape and bruise along the way has been worth it.
I didn't go through the fire just to quit now, to shrink from the gut wrenching pain that tried to destroy me.
No, I'm taking the memory of every disappointment, each heartbreak, all the things and people that hurt me at some time in my life and I'm using those things to fuel my drive to keep rising, growing stronger and flying high.
I'll not let anything in the life dissuade me from my path and I know now that I can overcome anything.
Bring on the fire- I burn even hotter with the passions of a unstoppable spirit.
It took me a while to understand that I can get through anything that life throws at me and that pain does heal, so I don't let the struggle bring me down anymore.
I face each challenge and every heartache head on and while it may hurt, it may linger for a while, I'll make it through one way or another…
I do every time.
I'm not just a survivor, I'm a thriver.

I'm a warrior with a heart of gold and an iron spirit.
And I got this.
I always will.

I'll Rise Up Better Every Time

Come on World, is that all you've got?
You've been trying to take me down for so long, and still, you think you can beat me?
No chance.
I was built to go through the fire carrying the weight of the world on my shoulders and keep going, even stronger.
Keep coming at me and I'll keep getting up, dusting myself off and rising again, better every time.
Yeah, you knocked me down a time or two, but you can't keep me down.
I'm too strong, too resilient and too tough to let anyone or anything beat me.
You can't break me anymore; you've already done that.
You can't shatter my heart; I've been through that too many times.
You can't crush my dreams because I'm chasing them harder than ever.

Maybe every day isn't a win, and every moment isn't beautiful, but I seize my chances, appreciate my life and love who I am ....

Sure, there are days when everything goes wrong and I can do no right, but I figure it out and push forward.

I keep showing up, standing tall and refusing to accept defeat ....

It's not in my warrior blood, I only get stronger from the storms that wash others away.

So, you're not going to bring me down anymore, World.

I've been through the worst, and I've kept going with a smile on my face.

So, yeah, I'm waking up today feeling pretty invincible,

And I welcome anything you think you can throw at me.

I know I'll stumble and I'll fall, but I'll keep getting up and fighting my way to the top.

I'm not perfect, but today, I feel unstoppable, flaws, scratches, scars and all.

I'm just a person who doesn't know how to quit, and I'll never let anyone or anything bring me down.

It took me a lot of failures, a lot of mistakes and way too many bad choices to get here, but I'm still standing ....

And I'll keep rising up and fighting on ....

Strong, beautiful and free.

Confidence Is the Courage to Be Yourself

I took a long hard look in the mirror this morning and realized something:

I don't care anymore if anyone really likes me.

I've been tucking away and protecting parts of myself for fear of disapproval from other people for far too long.

I'm not going to live like that anymore.

No more toning myself down or watering down my personality.

Not being true to myself has done nothing but left me feeling empty inside.

I'm promising myself that, from now on, I'll be the best version of me .... and I won't care who has a problem with that.

My friends, my tribe, my people – they all know and love the quirky, sometimes loud, outspoken and thoughtful person I am.

If anyone else wants my hand in friendship or heart in love, they'd better be prepared to embrace all of me .... quirks, scars, flaws and all.

After all, those are the parts of me that make me amazing.

Sometimes, I'm a mess, sometimes I'm a rockstar, but I'm always one of a kind.

So, I'm done seeking approval from the rest of the world and listening to their opinions of who and what I should be.

This is my life, and I'm living it the way that I choose.

I've spent too long trying to be someone I was never meant to be, and I'm done with that noise.

It's going to take a lot of confidence and bravery at first to stand fully in the light without caring what everyone thinks ....
But I'll get there.
Maybe some won't like me, maybe some will, but I will be able to look myself in the mirror everyday knowing that I've shown up –
Real to my personality,
True to my values,
And brave enough to not care.
Maybe I'm weird,
Maybe I'm too sarcastic.
Maybe I'm a complete mess at times.
But what matters most to me and always will is showing up, standing up and speaking up.
The world needs more of those qualities:
Courageous and real voices to be heard and appreciated for their uniqueness.
I might not change the world or make history, but I'll always tackle each and every day the way I always should have.
My way.
Rain or shine, rise or fall, I can smile brightly knowing that I'm living my life authentically.
In the end, that's what matters:
Filling my soul with happiness, chasing my dreams and leaving my mark on the world,
One heart at a time ... starting with my own.

A Woman Who Can Be Alone is Powerful

Her journey has never been an easy one- in fact, she never really had a choice on who she became or where life led her.

She set off to chase dreams and find adventure and somewhere along the way, she ended up finding her strength instead.

She didn't choose to become strong or become brave, she just did what she had to do to keep going and some days, just survive her life.

Truthfully, she didn't know what she was doing most of the time or even how she'd make it through, but after the storms passed, she was always standing-strong and resilient.

She learned that sometimes, you learn more from the journey than the destination.

During those tough times where she forged her strength from the fire, she wouldn't depend on anyone or anything, for she knew she could handle it all herself.

People might call her headstrong or stubborn, and she'd just smile and carry on.

She took great pride in her independence and no one would change that.

Her friends would always push her to look for love, to find a partner because they cared about her and didn't want her to be alone.

But this fiery woman full of life and spirit had always been okay with being alone- in fact, she thrived on it.

She loved her people and enjoyed their company, but she didn't need someone else or for love to complete her or make her happy.

She found that long ago within herself and it was the best decision she had ever made.

So, when the suitors came calling and people asked why she wasn't with someone, the fire behind her eyes would roar to life.

"Because I'm happy just the way that I am."

She would never turn away what's meant to be, but she wasn't looking for anything.

She had found all she had needed in herself, the beauty of her life and the joy of being fully alive.

She let the universe decide who and what was meant for her and she'd keep living in the moment and being present.

That was what would always make her powerful indeed:

She had stopped surviving and started thriving...

Happy to be who she was, do what she wanted and never look back.
Her life, her choices.
She'd never settle for anything less.

Today, I Become the Storm

She's done looking back, questioning herself and dwelling on her mistakes.
She's rising like the dawn of a new day, brighter, stronger and more powerful than she's ever been.
All her life, she's battled, struggled and fought for everything's she's wanted...
She didn't get the breaks and help to climb the mountains that she faced.
She's more than a survivor, she's a warrior queen with a fiery spirit and a strong heart.
No longer will she allow others to take advantage of her and she's turning the page on a new chapter- today.
No more excuses, no more apologies.
This day has been a long time coming...
When she started fighting for her dreams and stopped settling for less than she deserves-
In love, in life and in all the things that matter.
She's casting aside the pain of her often broken heart and she's using that anguish as fuel for her to rise stronger from the ashes.

Sure, she's afraid and doesn't have all the answers, but she knows she doesn't have to...
She just has to get up, keep going and take each day and step one at a time.
Courage isn't the absence of fear, but the knowledge that some things are more important...
Her happiness, her life, her self-worth, her friends.
Those are worth any price and she's going to battle for what she believes in.
She's been beaten down, dragged through failure and broken more times than she can remember...
But those challenges never defined her...
They forged her will in the fires that tried to consume her.
The flames made her the warrior she is.
Her time is now and she's rising.
She's taking back her life and her voice will be heard with resounding passion and conviction.
This day is long overdue and she's seizing it with both hands and standing in front of the storms that sought to bring her to her knees.
She's stared adversity, disaster and failure in the eyes before....
But now, she's not wavering any more.
She's strong, she believes and she knows she will continue to rise.
She has but a single thought as she charges forth into the struggles and fires that once almost ruined her and convinced her that she couldn't withstand the fury of life:
"Today, I become the storm...."

The Pain In Her Eyes & The Fire In Her Heart

She was strong because that was her only option.
She didn't know how to be anything else, and she was a survivor.
Her heart was hidden behind walls, because that's how she endured the pain,
that's how she faced the world behind a happy facade.
She tucked away the tears behind her smile, hid the pain underneath her laughter.
Her soulful eyes spoke a very different story, if you took the time to get past her deeply woven countenance of enigmatic mystery.
Most never did, and she was fine with that.
She loved her life and always on her terms.
She was a strong woman who had fought brokenness, failures and broken hearts.
A girl with dreams became a survivor with scars.

Her wounds didn't define her or defeat her, they forged her character and evolved het with each step or stumble...
Her broken road built her strength.
Her cracks of hard times eventually became the ways the light illuminated her soul.
The fire would never claim her.
Instead, she became a fiery Phoenix that continued to rise time and again.
There were those times, though,
When the sadness overwhelmed her and the tears became part of her story.
The silence at night could deafen her with the onslaught of emotions that tried to overwhelm her.
She wasn't the bravest or most beautiful,
But she was determined to become the most unforgettable and unstoppable.
She used her failures as fuel,
And her pain as motivation,
To never be broken again, but instead to let her light shine through the healed fissures of her heart.
She was a volatile tempest of emotions,
A magnificent mess and beautiful disaster,
But she was always true to herself.
Most would say she was the happiest of women,
But that was because they didn't know her sorrows or take the time to truly understand her...after all, depth scares some people away.
No one would want that burden- or so she thought.

She soon realized that the truest of loves, whether friends or soulmates, would always embrace her worst baggage....
And help her unpack.
She discovered that joy works better in twos,
But she didn't know if she could trust another man after the countless disappointments.
Her heart had been crushed so many times and her hopes had crumbled away,
She had once stopped finding reasons to believe in true love again...
Until some long forgotten stardust somehow sprinkled itself onto her soul.
The reason, against all odds and without reason, found her even as she believed she wasn't worthy of love.
Until she learned to truly love herself, she didn't know how to open her heart to another.
She knew the sun would always rise and maybe, just maybe. there was hope for a brighter tomorrow.
She knew that somewhere beyond all the storms,
There was a rainbow waiting just for her,
She realized that it was always darkest before dawn....
And it was time for the rise of her new day, the start of a new chapter.
On a blustery day, as it fate would have it, around a random corner, a curious thing happened on the way to forever.
Real and lasting love smiled on her...

And she never looked back.
She didn't know where tomorrow might lead, all she knew is that,
Finally, for the first time in as long as she could remember...
she had hope...
And she wasn't going to let it go...
With fire in her heart and passion in her soul,
There wasn't anything that could stop her now.
It was finally...
Her time to rise.

She Never Quit

I'm never going to be the flashiest, the loudest or even the most fashionable.
But my most remarkable qualities are hidden far below in my depths, far too valuable for those who don't deserve to know the real me.
My people- the ones who get me and truly love me- understand that I'm a warrior queen that won't be defeated or give up.
Yes, I've been down that road where I got knocked down, beaten up and forgotten.
But I wasn't ever meant to be the person to stay down or stop.
The fires of my life taught me one thing:
If I choose to be, I am unstoppable...
So that's what I became, each and every day.
I don't care if it's a challenge, a person or an achievement, I'm not stopping until I overcome or obtain it.
I'm not living my life in "what ifs" or "maybes".
I have dreams and goals that I won't be denied in realizing.

Yeah, I know it's going to hurt, I'm going to struggle and probably fall down a few times...
But I'm going to keep getting back up, coming back harder and finding a way to push forward.
While everyone else is shackled by their cants and not possibles, I'm fueled by the knowledge that I can do anything.
It won't always be pretty, but success is often dirty and messy...
But it's always worth it.
And so am I.
If you want to be a part of my life, be real, be true and most of all, be passionate.
I don't live or love halfway, so bring your best if you want to run with me.
I don't care if you're a friend or partner, it's all the same to me.
Intense, powerful and genuine...
That's who I am and how I live my life.
I was born to be a warrior and then I learned how to be strong.
So, if you ever hear my story and what I've overcome, it will always be about one thing:
No matter the odds or the struggle...
I never quit.
And I never, ever will

Cheer Me On While I Save Myself

I know you showed up wanting to be the knight in shining armor that saves the day and rescues the maiden, but this isn't that kind of story.
I'm not saying you can't be heroic and amazing, but I don't need be saved, completed or fixed.
I just need someone who'll stand beside me through the tough times when I'm fighting to make myself better and I'm doing my best to love myself.
Truth is, I would love someone to hold my hand and cheer me on when the going gets hard, because I'll need all the support I can get.
Maybe it's not the fairy tale ending you had planned, but it's real, it's genuine and it's the kind of love that lasts.
We don't live in a world of glass slippers and swashbuckling, and I don't want or need a hero.
I need someone to be real with me when the world gets hard.

I want someone who can love me when I'm not easy to love.
I need someone who will stand beside me, be strong and sometimes carry the load when it gets too heavy for me.
It doesn't mean that I'm weak or can't handle life....just that every so often, I get tired.
Not because I need more sleep, but because sometimes, I'm just weary.
So if you really want to be a hero, those are the times you can step up, shoulder the load and let me rest for a a moment.
Let me take a breath so I can come back stronger and better.
Because in the end, it'll be you and me versus the world.
It's not your job to do it all and there's going to be times when I need a hand.
Together, we can get through it all.
I know it's hard for you to stand aside and let me fight my battles, but I can overcome anything that comes at me.
Let me do what I have to do, struggle and rise again because you can't go there for me...
And I don't want you to.
Let me be the person I'm working hard to become and be my biggest cheerleader like I'll always be for you.
Because sometimes, at the end of a long hard day, it's just a great thing to just hear you say "way to go" with a long hug.

When it's all said and done, I don't need a hero or a knight in shining armor.
I just want you to be my safe place to lay my head....where my heart will always be safe.
That's my best version of happily ever after.

Never Mistake Her Quietness For Weakness

All her life, she's been underestimated, taken for granted and disrespected...
And there was a time that she overlooked her mistreatment and rationalized the bad behavior of others.
Not anymore.
She's done being too nice and allowing others to treat her poorly.
She couldn't tell you what happened to cause her to reach her breaking point, but she has...
And all the selfish people, toxic behavior and negativity....she's turning and walking the other way from all that noise.
She's not allowing anyone to disrespect her any longer.
She was never weak, she just made excuses for people that never deserved them or her.
Those same people have a choice:

Either accept the new her that she's decided to become...
Or make their way out of her life.
No, today is the start of a new chapter in her life.
She's turning the page and leaving behind the bad stuff that once dragged her down and tainted her life.
She's choosing to rise above the storm, fight for what she wants and deserves and to never stop chasing her dreams.
She knows the road of change is hard and the climb will be steep,
But she also knows that she is worth it.
She's worth it all.
Maybe it took her longer than most to come into her own, but now that she's beginning to uncover those hidden parts of her that have been dormant too long...
And like the hurricane , her life and her mindset is slowly transforming...
Her once still air of complacency is quickly erupting into the force of a woman that will not be stopped...
She is strong and she is finally taking back her power...
She knows she can do what it takes to reclaim her happiness.
And one more thing:
She is me...
And my time is now.

I'm Worth It - I Always Will Be Worth It.

I know you thought that I would just be another challenge for you, and that's true…
I am challenging.
That's just the start of who I am.
There's so much more to me than you could never have expected, and that's okay.
Most people aren't prepared for a person like me- I possess an uncommon fire and passion that is unparalleled…
And I can't be diminished or dismissed, no matter how hard you try.
But what you also didn't count on was that I'm not just another pretty face or notch in your belt…
Far from it, in fact.
I'm the one that you were told to wait for....but I'm also the one you were warned about.
You've never met one like me and you never will again, so forget what you know and lose the player's guide that you follow.

There are only two options with me:
Make me a priority or find another choice…
Because I don't play waiting games and I'm not going to chase you.
I know my worth and I value my self-respect…
And if you can't do the same, then let's part amicably.
I'm never going to be the one begging for your attention, playing the games or being okay with being ignored.
I'll never tell you that I'm perfect, flawless or without fault, because I have my bad days, fits of emotional outbursts and even the times when I don't really want to leave the house.
But even with my complicated and sometimes messy self, I'm worth everything.
I'm worth being put first.
I'm worth being treated with respect.
I'm worthy of being loved the way I deserve.
Maybe you're the one I've been waiting for and perhaps you're up to the task…
Time will tell and actions will speak volumes.
Don't tell me what you're going to do or how…
Just do it…
With class, honor, respect and character.
Who knows?
Play your cards right and I might just end up on your arm.
It's up to you to prove that you're worth it.
I know I am.

I'm Perfectly Flawed, and I Like It

I realize that I can be an absolute mess at times, it's just part of who I am.

I wish I could tell you that I was a simple person, but I'm anything but.

I'm a complex personality with a unique blend of qualities that may make your head spin sometimes.

At first glance, people think I'm a strong person, but those who really understand and love me know I'm a deep-feeling soul with a loving heart .... and I'm weak when it comes to the people I care about.

I know I'm not easy to understand, and I appreciate my people who get that I'm worth the effort.

I used to think I was an introvert, but the more I learned about myself the more I realized that I'm a little bit extrovert too .... it all just depends on my mood and who I'm with.

There are days when I feel like pulling my hair out and crying minutes before something hilarious makes me double over with side-splitting laughter.

That's the beautiful disaster that is me – you never know which version you'll get, and you may even get both at the same time, so buckle up, Buttercup .... I'm always a heck of a ride.

Some may say I'm challenging, but I just call it interesting.

Anyone can be ordinary, average and routine ... I keep things a bit on the spicy side, though I don't do it that way on purpose.

You'll never really know what's going through my mind; I've learned to disguise my emotions masterfully – I'll often tell you that I don't care when the truth is I care too much.

I have the simple needs most people have – to love and be loved, to be understood and appreciated ....

I just happen to pursue those desires in extraordinary ways ....

With sass, pizzazz, and a lot of sarcasm sometimes too.

I call that my bold, fun flavor – tasty to those who love me and disconcerting to the rest ....

But I realized a long time ago that I would never be able to please everyone.

So, I stopped trying.

Better to make myself happy, fill my soul with joy and love my life and my people with all my heart.

If I can't put my whole heart and soul into something or someone, I'll do what's best for me and step away.

I know I'm awesome in all my flaws, and I embrace each of my dents, imperfections and scars fully.

They've made me who I am, and I'll never regret anything I've done or anywhere I've been.
I'm a big bundle of emotions, happiness and personality, and you'll never forget me once we've met.
Maybe you'll love me, maybe not ....
But I'll keep on dancing to my own beat, living in my own light and loving myself the best way I know how.
I like who I am, and I guess it's up to you to decide if you do too ....
I'll keep on doing what I do best regardless.
Shining brightly.

Stronger For The Struggle

My story is a tale of failure and falling,
A time when I didn't know if I could ever find my strength again.
When you're on your knees trying to muster the courage to stand again, everything seems impossible.
Nothing is easy when you're down and out, and everywhere you turn, you find only disappointment.
From broken hearts to broken roads, it's easy to get lost in the battle for survival.
Moments turned into memories and before I knew it, I was buried beneath the faded dreams of yesterday.
Truth is, though, it's in those moments when the fires of struggle threaten to tear your spirit apart that you make a choice...
Choose to lose yourself in the flames of misery or face the heat and become the fire...
Rise again and be reborn the phoenix from the ashes of a painful past.
Sometimes, you find your strength when being strong is the only option you have.

Forged in the flames of fiery trials, I refused to let my failures define me.
I knew that to survive, to become stronger and better, I had to transform my tragedy into triumph.
No excuses, settling or halfway efforts.
The best way to dig out of a hole is to do it with all your heart, filled with passion and motivated by pain.
I couldn't always see the light of better days and there are still days that I want to quit,
But I know I'm better than that.
I deserve more than that.
I'll never let bad days and hard times define me or destroy me.
This is my life and my choice, and I choose to live my life with relentless optimism and zealous courage.
I won't be reduced, defined or defeated by the people and the past that tried to destroy me.
The fire burning in my heart can't be quenched and I won't accept anything or anyone in my life who doesn't accept me for the brokenly beautiful person that I am.
I don't need anyone's pity, handout or sympathy…
I just want their best, all the time in all the ways.
Love me or leave me, I'll always be respected and appreciated…
On my terms, no more and no less.
Yes, my struggles scared and scarred me, but those are just the reminders of where I've been, not where I'm going.

I'm not who I was and I'm not yet who I am meant to be, but that's the beauty of writing my own story:
I can create every chapter of my life just the way I want in the way I choose.
No matter where I go and what I do, whenever you meet me, you'll realize one thing about me.
I'll never be complacent, ordinary or lackluster...
In all the ways that matter to all the people
who I care about-
Heart, spirit and soul...
I'll always be on fire for being alive.

I Fought Hard to Become the Person I Am.

I'll never forget the words of all the people who never believed in me along the way.
The ones that counted me out when everything went bad- they became the reasons that I used to fuel my fire.
Their words, their lack of support and belief in me gave me the drive every day to rising again and keep fighting...
To keep showing up and getting stronger and wiser every step of the way.
Honestly,
There were times that I didn't think I'd survive and challenges I never thought I could overcome...
But I did.
And I kept doing.
I kept hearing their words and I pushed harder, battled harder.
I stopped simply surviving, found my sword and attacked life back...

I plunged in, headfirst, and fought to break free of the mindset and the place that was holding me back.
You know what?
I didn't always win.
I still got knocked down and fell apart more times than I can remember.
But that's the thing about a strong person…
We never stay down.
We find a way to believe.
We keep going.
So now, when I look in the mirror, I don't see that broken person that used to stare back at me through tired eyes and a weary heart.
No, I see someone much different.
A brave, capable and unstoppable spirit that I've grown to love.
Not because I'm perfect or have it all figured out.
No, because I know the price I've paid to become her and the battles I've fought to be the person I set out to be.
Few will ever know my journey or my reasons why I made the choices I did, and I'm good with that...
Because they'll never forget my courageous fire, and if they're lucky, they'll never have to.
I love me-and if I choose to let them,
They will too.

She's A Butterfly with Bullet Holes In Her Wings…

They judged her because they thought they knew her- only, they had no clue who she really was.
She was a rare creature that had managed to fly high in spite of all the things that had tried to take her down.
The world would see her failures and her falls, thinking she'd stay down on rock bottom.
What they didn't know about this woman was that the same fire that had tried to destroy her had also forged her courage and bravery.
She wasn't content to let the storms douse her fiery will- far from it.
She always knew who she was and what she could do…and she wasn't content to let her failures define her.
Midst the chaos that was once her life, she had found her wings and despite everything stacked against her, she started to learn to fly.

No one gave her a chance and well, she was accustomed to that- she had never been given anything in her life except a choice to fight her way out of the anguish she once knew.

She earned each step she took with the signs of her strength-scars, scratches and bruises that forged her indomitable spirit.

Sure, she fell from the skies more times than she could count and had to pick herself up much of the time...

But she persevered, because her story never gave her any other choice.

Day by day, step by step, she began to soar higher with each opportunity...

Flying high with the courage, fire and fight that characterized exactly who she was...

And with the grace of the beautiful soul that she was, she just kept smiling and shining...

For she was one of those remarkable people you never forget.

Always strong, beautiful and free...

Now, she was flying high too...

And she never looked back.

The Deeper The Pain, The Stronger the Wings

She's battled the hardest fights life could throw at her and the weight of the world weighs heavily on her. She's only ever had herself to depend on, so she doesn't look to anyone else to help ease her burden. Whatever you want to call her- broken, a mess, lost- she doesn't care, because she stopped worrying about what others thought a long time ago.
She's been to rock bottom too many times and picked herself up more times than she can count.
She's not trying to be strong, a survivor or anything else, she is just trying to keep going.
She's tired of suffering without an end in sight. Truthfully, she found herself in the darkness when she couldn't find anything else- not even the light. She didn't know how she'd survive the broken failure that was her life, but somehow, painfully, she did.
She clawed her way out of the abyss and slowly, she began to build her resolve.
It was never about flying high or succeeding to her, it was just about finding some peace in a world that never gave her a chance.

No one ever expected her to rise from the ashes, so when they saw her pulling herself out of the emotional wreckage of her life, they were stunned.

They didn't know her life or her story, nor did they know her reasons...

They never knew that this scarred and flawed angel never wanted wings....she just wanted to breathe free.

Reeling from the pain and digging deep to find her courage, she uncovered the parts of herself that she never knew existed.

She wasn't trying to be a hero or a role model, she was just trying to survive a story that didn't give her any other choice...

She was broken.

She was lost.

She was counted out.

She rose again...

And using the pain to fuel the fires of her passion, she became something else entirely.

A warrior forged of fire and scarred by pain, she would never again let anyone hurt her so deeply, she vowed with the beautiful countenance of a strong woman who has walked through hell....and kept smiling.

As she broke free of the shackles of struggle that once held her down, she gleefully stepped into the light that had eluded her for so long...

In that moment, she found herself, finally, at a place she'd never known....but had long dreamt of...

And as she stepped into the dawn of a new chapter, out sprung wings she'd never cared a thing to have, but yet, she was always meant to possess...
But, finally having the courage and strength to fly high, she finally reached that place she had wanted to find as long as she could remember...
A place she'd sought her entire life-
Where she was, at least, free....free to breathe deeply and free to fly high.
So that's just what she did...
And she never looked back.

Behind Every Strong Person Is a Child Who Never Quit Chasing Their Dreams

I made a promise to myself that I would never give up on my dreams.
There were a lot of times that I lost my way, couldn't see the light and didn't know where to go next.
I thought the magic of finding your dreams was in reaching your destination, but that's not true at all.
Every misstep, bad decision and poor choice led me down the road I needed to take to build a stronger character, forge a brave spirit and learn what I was capable of.
I often wondered why I struggled so much and why so many things went wrong, but that's what I needed to experience to become the person I am today.
I went through the fire to understand how to rise again.
I failed and stumbled so I could learn how to pick myself back up and keep going.

I chose the wrong people to love so I could figure out how to be cautious in my choices.

I thought I had lost my magic and my way so many times that I didn't think I'd ever get where I was trying to go.

But that's the funny thing about life …

It gives you what you need, when you need it …. but it doesn't always give you what you want.

But that's ok.

My goals and dreams don't have expiration dates, and there's no hurry to make things happen.

I've learned that people enter your life for a reason, a season or a lesson, and I've made the most of that knowledge.

I've found my tribe, my people, and I know that I'm never alone.

I've made it this far without always knowing where I was going because I never lost sight of who I wanted to become.

I valued the things that matter most to me: passion, character, authenticity and love.

Maybe they call me a dreamer, but I'm not the only one.

I've got light in my eyes and fire in my heart, so there's nothing I can't do if I put my mind to it.

I've been knocked down, failed and fallen, but I've never stopped believing in myself or my dreams.

Life isn't always grand or full of big moments, but I've learned to treasure the little things along the way: a beautiful friendship, a kind compliment, a warm drink on a chilly morning .... There's beauty all around, and I've finally stopped rushing and started taking it all in. There's no reason to hurry through life and miss all the little things that bring joy.

I know that I can realize my dreams while loving myself and my life .... just the way I want.

Each and every day, I'll keep enjoying the journey, living my best life and loving myself and my people. In the end, it's not about the number of breaths we take, but the moments that take our breath away .... Starting with today.

A Strong Woman Picks Up The Pieces

She's not always the person that speaks the loudest, walks the proudest or seems the strongest.
But beneath her layers of steely facade and happy smiles, there is a heart of gold and an iron will.
She's been through the fire more than once, but every time, she found a way and kept going.
She never really was given another option....so she did what she had to do to survive...
And once she got better at surviving, she started thriving and growing.
Instead of always reacting to the storms that threatened to bring her down, she started taking charge of her life and her destiny.
Most would meet her without ever realizing they had crossed paths with one of the most beautiful souls and strongest people that they would ever meet...
And they didn't have to know.
She was proud and strong, but in a quiet and unassuming way that just kept pushing forward.

No spotlight or fanfare, just an amazingly strong woman who decided she would never give up, stay down or be a victim.
This was her life and she chose to live it to its fullest- bad days, great times and everything in between.
Truthfully, she never had all the answers or knew where her days would take her....quite the opposite.
But what she did know was that she could overcome anything, against any odds and still be smiling on the other side.
There's just something remarkably beautiful about a soul that doesn't know how to quit...
Each time she fell, she got up stronger than before with more determination than she had started with.
She carries the weight of the world for herself and the people she loves, and she does it without a second thought.
That's just who she is-
Friend, lover, sister, mother and everything else in between.
You can't define her because her role is constantly adapting to whatever she needs to be in the moment.
So, when you see her smile, understand that her depths are complex, her strength is undeniable and that beneath all the layers of complexity is a unstoppable person that will always keep getting up,
Keep fighting back harder,
And always, she'll be radiating brightly as she battles and shines through it all.
From the ashes to her ascension, she's always going to keep rising higher like the Phoenix that she is.

My Story is One of Triumph & Tragedy

Yes, I went down the wrong roads and made all the bad choices,
I ended up in places I never should have been-in ways that tore my spirit apart.
Truth be told, I don't know how I got so down and out,
Nor how I made it out intact and still whole.
At the end of my rope and hating who I'd become,
I hit rock bottom.
Everyone counted me out and no one gave me a chance....
Even I didn't know how to dig myself out of the hole...
But you know,
That's the thing about a spirit that won't give up.
I don't know how to quit and I'm meant to become more in spite of my rough start.
It was never meant to be the end of my story, I just had to begin a new chapter- one where the Phoenix rises from the ashes.

I pulled myself up, dusted myself off then fought and clawed my way back.
I didn't ask for help and no one offered me a hand, but that was what I needed to forge my own courage and build my own strength.
My dreams didn't have an expiration and I wasn't going to quit on them or myself.
I know I'm a mess sometimes,
A bit of a broken soul with glimpses of beauty stashed in between,
But I'm good with that.
I made my way, earned my place and I'm fighting to make my story a success.
I've got a lot of love to give and a passionate fire that can't be quenched.
Sometimes, you realize along the way that you don't set out to be strong and courageous,
But when you're
left holding the pieces of a life gone wrong,
Those are the only choices you have left.
It's not that I'll ever be heroic, strong and amazing like the fabled stories of heroes and lovers,
But at least I'll write my story my way, and that's what matters most of all.
I don't have to set the world on fire, just be on fire for my life-
The kind of flames that make your heart and soul feel totally alive.
I may be beautifully broken and wonderfully imperfect,

But I'm still standing.
I'm still strong.
I figured where I needed to go and what it would take to get there, so I made a choice:
I didn't ever go looking for a hero-
I decided instead to become the hero of my own story...
One small victory at a time...my way...

The Price of Becoming Who You Are

Most people who meet her see a strong person, capable of overcoming anything ....
They'll never realize the price she had to pay to become the person that she is.
She started off much differently – bright eyed and hopeful, she charged into the world with her heart on her sleeve and light in her eyes ....
But life tried to take all that away from her, it did everything it could to bring her to her knees.
What the world didn't know was that behind the thoughtful eyes and dreamer spirit was a fighter – a brave soul who wouldn't accept defeat and refused to let hardship tear her apart.
While she still made bad choices and suffered crushing heartbreak, she never pitied herself nor wallowed in her failures.
She was better than that, for she knew the challenges that lie in front of her and refused to let life bring her down.

Maybe she wasn't ready for the fire that scorched her soul, perhaps she didn't know how hard her journey would become – loss and pain can destroy some – but she never let her mistakes define her path.

She had promised herself from the very beginning never to lose sight of the things and people that mattered to her.

She managed to balance her outward toughness with a sensitive and loving heart in a world that doesn't easily let you be both.

That doesn't mean she didn't struggle with hard days or get down on herself, for there were days that she had to dig deep and claw her way through to the end .... but she always kept going.

Maybe she got frustrated a time or two, perhaps she cried a little when she felt overwhelmed sometimes, but you'd never be able to tell ....

For her beautifully placid eyes were the symbol of who she was and the hardy spirit that pushed her to keep getting up and looking up.

So, when the fires of life raged around her, she didn't just keep walking through the flames .... she became the fire.

When everyone else quit, she found a way to keep going and rising above – for she refused to quit or accept failure.

She was an unusual blend of a beautiful soul with both claws to dig herself out of the harshest battles and wings to fly high and chase her dreams.

She wasn't just a woman; she was a fighter with an unrelenting vision to become everything she ever wanted to be ....
And so that's the path she chose, rain or shine.
She kept showing up, stepping up and rising again.
One moment, one day and one dream at a time ....
She kept believing and evolving.
Beautiful, strong and free.

There is Nothing Greater Than A Self Made Woman

She's had to grow stronger when she didn't think she could, hold it together when she was falling apart and fight to keep going when she didn't think it was possible.

She became more than a survivor, she transformed into a warrior.

She didn't rely on loud and brash words to make her way through the world...

No, she did it with a quiet confidence and stolid countenance that belies her fierce nature.

She's not passive, mild or meek- far from it, though you may not know it at first glance.

Her sly smile may lead you to think she's anything but what she truly is-

A strong woman determined to rise against all odds and any challenge,

For that is who she has become and the fire that she forged from the ashes she rose from.

She's been through more than most people will ever know and she knows what it means to keep going when everyone else would quit.
She doesn't know how to fail and staying down isn't in her blood...
She learned a long time ago to depend only on herself, so that's what she did as she kept growing, building and evolving.
They'd wonder aloud how she always managed to turn setbacks into comebacks and seemingly found a way when there wasn't one.
She was so many things to so many people but she would forever be proud of who she grew to become:
Strong woman, independent spirit and brave soul.
Beneath the quiet facade was an extraordinary woman with zealous passion, fiery heart and courageous drive...
And she touched lives and brightened the day wherever she went.
She burned with the intensity of a roaring wildfire and shined with the sparkle of the brightest night sky...
An unassuming woman who could conquer or overcome anything.
And nothing or no one would ever take that away from her.
Because there was a confidence in her silence and a strength in her smile that couldn't be denied...
And there's nothing more powerful than a self-made woman...
That's exactly what she was-
And she made sure no one ever forgot that

Being Remembered For My Strength

All my life, people have called me difficult, stubborn and feisty and the list goes on.
And every time someone tries to fit me into a box because I won't live my life by their rules, I just smile.
I learned a long time ago in the hardest way possible that if you do what they want and try to please people, they're still going to talk about you anyways.
So, I'm going to dance to my own music, do the things that make me happy and oh yes, refuse to let anyone try to make me feel less than I deserve.
I'm strong enough, I'm worthy of love and I work hard to be a good person, so forgive me if I don't care what you call me.
Life's too short and joy can be too fleeting to let anyone walk all over me.
My voice will be heard.
I will not be disrespected.
I will stand up for myself and others that can't.
I'm going to keep putting love out in the world, because the way I see it,

There's already too much ugliness out there now.
So, yeah, I'm never going to be the quiet one, the one to blend in or follow the crowd.
I don't care about attention or notoriety, I just want to happy and live a full life...
On my terms.
No one else has the right to tell me how to he, how to look or who to love.
Sure, they'll shake their heads and call me difficult.
But I'm proud of who I am and the person I'm becoming.
After it's all said and done,
I just want to be remembered for being authentic and real...
After all, anyone can fall for almost anything, but it takes someone special to stand up for what matters to them.
That's me.
Strong, proud and free.

A Self Renovation

That me that you used to know?
Yeah, that person is gone now.
I had a lot of stuff weighing me down, and I couldn't keep going the way that I was ....
So, I did the hardest thing I've ever done and renovated myself – improved, evolved and grew the parts that needed to catch up to the me that I want to be.
Yes, that's right. You probably won't recognize this version of me anymore, because it's way better than that disaster that I used to be ....
Going from mistake to mistake and loving all the wrong people .... I'm amazed I'm still in one piece.
But here I am, renovated, elevated and dedicated to improving myself.
No, I'm not going to let you or anyone else treat me the way that you used to – I'm better than that, and I deserve more.
I'm raising the bar, my standards and my head as I start changing the game in my favor.
I'm tired of losing at life, falling flat on my face and feeling hopeless all the time.

So, excuse me if I don't have time for people who used to disrespect me, mistreat me or brush me aside.

If you want to step to my new level, then you'll need a taller ladder this time.

I'm still the same wonderful soul behind my fiery eyes, but now, I'm expecting more, giving more and never giving up.

Maybe you can handle that, maybe you can't.

Either way, I'm going to keep evolving to get better every day ....

So, I know you think you know me, but I can promise you that I'm not the person you knew.

I'm stronger.

I'm wiser.

And I'm so much better than I ever was before.

Change is inevitable, but evolution is optional .... So, I chose to evolve.

What are you choosing?

My Story

Looking back, I'll never tell you it was easy to get to where I am today..
I am far from where I want to be and I have much still left to learn and understand about myself and life.
It's been a long and hard journey that has taken everything I have,
And truthfully,
Most days I don't know how I survive.
I get knocked down and kicked around until I think I can't go on..
But I do and always have..
You do it long enough that survival mode becomes a way of life.
Honestly, I've done most of the damage to myself with bad decisions and self doubt,
But that's just part of the process, I guess.
I never thought I'd learn to rise above and find my way,
But I did and I still am, every day.
And I'm still learning- I have far yet to go.

I have days that take everything I've got to survive and nights that seem to never end.
I've been a horrible person but I've also chosen to do good things too.
I'm flawed, broken and messed up...
But I also have a big heart, beautiful thoughts and a kind spirit...
And it's a battle between both sides, every day.
I have more good days than bad now, but it's still hard.
I don't win as much as I lose,
But that's okay.
I'm learning, I'm growing and I'm trying to be better today than I was yesterday.
I can't ever take back all the pain I've caused and I can't undo the wrong I've done...
But I'm trying to make amends, rebuild trust and maybe in time, be a good person...
Or at least feel good about where I am in my journey.
I don't like what I see in the mirror and haven't in a long time...
But there are glimpses of hope every so often.
I know it'll take time, but I'm working on it- working on me, one day at a time the best that I can.
So, maybe some day when you see me finally flying high and shining brightly,
I'll tell you the story of how I found my wings...
It won't be a tale of glorious victory and dazzling dreams...

No, it'll be a story of failure, darkness and fighting to get better and be stronger.
It won't be shiny and happy, but it'll be real...
And it'll be me.
And in the end, that's what will matter most in my journey:
That I battled, kept going and found my way.
Overcame my failures and learned from my mistakes.
Maybe it'll be a beautiful day, that day when I tell you that story.
Maybe not.
But it will be real.
And that's the kind of stuff that matters.
The painful hard truths that get us where we need to be.
One glorious but messy day at a time.

I Overcame Everything and Kept Going

I know that everyone has a story and I'm no different. I'm sure there are worse tales of tragedy and triumph, but that doesn't diminish my struggles or take away from my accomplishments.

Maybe people won't think that my journey isn't all that remarkable, but they didn't walk beside me during those hard times and fight the battles that tried to take me down.

I know the price I paid to get where I am and the sacrifices I made along the way...

And that's what matters most to me:

Remembering where I started and how far I've come. The fires that tried to burn down my life don't overwhelm me anymore because I learned to use that pain and strife to fuel my passions and spark my drive.

I do this for me and the people I love.

I find a way every day to do all the things for everyone else and still have a little left over for me to enjoy a few moments of contemplative introspection. There's no fanfare or trophy for what I do and there doesn't have to be.

I choose this path and this life…

And I'll keep choosing it every day in every way.

The way I overcome the challenges is a testament to my unending courage and battle tested bravery.

I'm proud of who I've worked hard to become and all the things I've fought to achieve.

I could've given up so many times and stayed down, but that's not who I am or will ever be.

I'm a warrior with a heart of gold and a soul full of depth….nothing in this life is too much for me and there's no obstacle I can't overcome.

So, one day when I'm nothing more than a beautiful memory of strength and resiliency, I want them to speak of me in inspired tones with heroic words of valor and grit.

That I never gave up or gave in and I paid every price that I had to in order to keep pushing forward.

That I overcame everything and kept going, fighting and evolving.

I want my story to be one of a kind…

One where I loved hard when there was love to be had, fought bravely when I had to and never gave up on anyone or anything.

That in the end, for my people, my life and my dreams, I gave it all I had…

And that made all the difference between ordinary and extraordinary.
That will be my legacy...
And I'm proud to say I did it all my way...

She Won't Apologize For Her Strength

She used to water down her large personality and strong will to try to fit in.
The men would say she was intimidating, hard to handle or just too much...
And that was true-
She was too much of all the things that matter most: Personality, passion, love, soul, strength...
She was only too much for those who couldn't handle her and she soon realized that making herself less to help others feel more just made her feel bad about herself,
So she decided to stop filtering, holding back or being anything other than who she was...
And she never felt better in her life.
Maybe everyone didn't like her truths and maybe she was too much for some people, but she was good with that.
Those people shouldn't be in her life if she was overwhelming to them.

Her people- the ones that loved and supported her- enjoyed every bit of her unfiltered and raw spirit.

She was a blessing to those who loved her and a fierce woman those who didn't understand her.

Love would never be worth settling, sacrificing or making do with less than she deserved, and she knew that.

She didn't have all the answers and most of the time, flew by the seat of her pants, but she loved and lived passionately in the way that made her happy...

And after all that time trying to dial down who she truly was, she finally felt free and unencumbered by the expectations and needs of those who didn't matter.

She stopped making apologies to those who couldn't handle her strength and started embracing who she truly was.

Maybe it was a little harder standing out the way she did, but she'd rather live her life honestly than to pretend to be what she wasn't.

This was her life and she didn't have to justify who and what she was to anyone...

Especially the ones who tried to judge her choices without understanding her reasons.

They didn't know her and she didn't care if they did... she knew who she was and that would always be what mattered most to her.

She was perfectly content to take each day as it came and she would never change for anyone other than herself.

She won't ever be perfect, flawless or easy to love,
but she liked what she was better, anyways:
Beautiful, strong and free...
And she was happy just the way she was.
Always.

My Scars Tell My Story

I learned long ago that you can't always see every scar- some are much deeper than superficial skin wounds…
The emotional scars of heartache or hurtful words sometimes don't ever fully heal,
But they're still there as a reminder…
Of times that life took its best shot at me, trying to hurt me and bring me down-
But never could.
Maybe I can't run my hands over those kinds of scars, but they're still there and still hurt in their own way.
Other people can't see those but they don't have to-
Most wouldn't understand the story behind those deepest kinds of scars.
But I do.
I can think back to how I felt and how it hurt when those scars ache just a bit..
But that's when I close my eyes and remember how far I've come, how much stronger I've become and the person that I am now.
Yeah, I got beat up and it was a hard time, but those

scars are all there for a reason-
They remind me that I can get through anything and I always will.
I'm much more than a survivor, I'm a warrior.
I love deeply and live passionately.
Maybe I fall down and make mistakes, but that's just part of the journey- the parts that I learn and grow from.
I know that tomorrow will come and with each day, I become a better person..
And that's what matters most to me.
Being better than I was yesterday.
And those scars?
They just remind me of where I've been so that I never go back.
Onward and upward, always.
Life is a beautiful journey..
And I'm going to enjoy it the best that I can,
One glorious step, moment and day at a time.

I Will Always Be on the Rise

I know you thought I was down and out, but I guess you don't really know me at all.
Yeah, I'm gonna get knocked down, dragged around and fall flat on my face sometimes...
But that's just part of life and I never stay down.
Those flames that threaten to tear me apart every day don't destroy me...
They strengthen me.
The passion that roars in my blood is stoked by the fires that I've survived.
I'm more than a survivor, much more.
I'm a warrior with a heart of gold and courage of a hurricane.
I can't be denied, stopped or turned away...
I'm not wired that way.
No matter what it takes or how hard the climb is, I will always rise again-
Each time, better, wiser and stronger than before.
So, I know you thought you could destroy me with your actions and break me with your words, but it will be the last time you underestimate me.

I'm not like the others before me.
You can't contain or tame the wildfire in my spirit or shackle the wild wind in my heart...
I'm more than just a woman, I'm unstoppable.
In every way, every day ... I just keep rising.
Maybe you thought you'd have the last laugh and my demise would be the ego boost you sought, but this is my notice to you:
I don't want you or anyone else in my life that will try to tear me apart.
I've already been broken more times than you will ever know-
And I'm still here, standing defiantly against the world and the people who would see me fail.
I've been through the worst and yet, I'm still going stronger than ever.
I make broken look beautiful in a way you'll never understand...
And you don't have to.
This is my life and my rules, so I'm doing what I do best.
Rising, evolving and getting stronger.
After all, broken girls evolve into the most unstoppable women.
And I didn't just learn how to dance in the rain...
I became the storm

She Was a Warm Embrace, His Reminder of Beauty in the World

No matter how hard life could be, she was always waiting for him, arms open –
The warm embrace at the end of a sometimes-cold day, reminding him that his safe place was forever in his arms.
Though they parted every morning to pursue their various endeavors, they never lost their beautiful connection, for they always carried their love with them, no matter how far they traveled.
A simple text, quick call or little nudges of love between them always kept their fire burning when the world tried to quench the spark.
There were always moments when life brought them to their knees, but together, hand in hand, they always found their way and their strength to push forward ....

Never losing their special bond, for that was the essence of their souls.

They both knew that she was his fire, and he was her rock, and their hearts beat as one, even as the world could come crashing down around them.

In a life that did everything to tear them apart and destroy their love, they always found each other and nurtured the beauty of their connection, each and every day.

Maybe it wasn't perfect or full of grandiose moments, but it was real, it was true, and more than anything,

It was the two of them, loving each other in their own special way.

Some of our love stories may be a little dented and scratched, but they're every bit as beautiful as the fairytales.

Because they're our own special love, told in a beautiful way that only we will know and appreciate. And that's the most wonderful part of all.

She Fought Her Own Battles

She'd learned the hard way she couldn't depend on anyone else.
She'd fought the hard battles, been knocked down more times than she could count and somehow, she always managed to find a way to survive.
Help?
Backup ?
Someone to rescue her?
She never had any of those things, so she stopped hoping for a knight in shining armor and started looking for her sword.
She didn't need to be saved, rescued or fixed...
She just needed to do what she did best- keep going , keep smiling and keep rising.
It wasn't easy- there were so many days that she wanted to quit, throw in the towel and give up...
But that wasn't who she was or ever would be.
Her strength and courage was forged in those same fires that once tried to burn her down.

Not only did she emerge from the flames scarred but stronger, but she learned a resilience that an easy path would have never taught her.

She reminded herself often that she was strong because of the challenges and that she could overcome anything if she just kept fighting...

So she did.

Through the heartbreaks, the disappointments, even the sadness from saying goodbye to people.

The ones meant for her would always find a way to stay in her life, so she learned to let the others go and hold her people tightly.

And love?

She would just smile at the men full of ego and bravado and move on.

They weren't there for her- they just sought to boost their own egos.

She would wait for the one who would be there, without expectation or demand, equal and loving....who knew she needed someone to run beside her, not try to tame her...

Because she didn't need a man to make her whole...she was already happy and complete, just the way she was.

She knew how to fight her own battles, make her own choices and love herself the way she wanted...

And anyone that wanted to win her heart?

They didn't need to bring a sword, armor or glorious words...

They just needed to be real and accepting.

In her story, she was the hero…and that's exactly how she planned to keep it.

A maiden forged in the flames and strong enough to stand alone.

She smiled.

Until she found one strong enough to stand beside her, she'd keep living life fully, loving her people passionately and rising high like she was meant to do.

But then, she was happy, just the way she was.

And in the end, that's what mattered most.

Her happily ever after started and ended the way it was supposed to:

With her.

Strong, fierce and free.

The Phoenix

She's strong because that's the only way she's survived her past.
She's been to rock bottom so many times, it started to feel too comfortable until she chose to break the cycle.
Until she decided enough was enough-and it was only after countless failures, falls to the bottom and broken hearts that she hit her limit.
She had a choice: succumb to the fires of her life or step up, rise up and become the fire.
Her soul was weary and her heart was tired but she didn't have any options-
Her life didn't give her one.
So, instead of wallowing, staying down and giving up, she did the only thing she knew to do:
She turned her setback into a comeback...
Only this time, she wasn't going to settle for returning to "normal."
She needed more than average, lackluster and ordinary.

She chose to rise from the ashes of rock bottom with an iron will, a warrior's spirit and the strength of a thousand suns.

She was done surviving and trying to manage her life....that had done nothing but landed her at rock bottom, time and again.

No, this time, she was fighting for more...

More of her life, her voice and most of all, her lost magic...

The part of her that she had lost along the way as life had tried to pummel the hope and dreams out of her...

But it failed.

She didn't know how or when she'd claw herself out of the darkness, only that she was determined to rise above, become stronger...

To find her wings.

She realized it was never truly about being perfect, she just needed to persevere-

Every day, in every way.

That was her ticket to the top.

Sure, she'd get some bumps and bruises along the way, but she was ready for that.

The question was....

Could life handle her best, because that's what she was bringing with her as she rose again.

No excuses, no miracles, no choices.

She was strong because her story gave her no other choice...

Only now, she was turning the page and starting a new chapter called simply:
The Phoenix.

The Strongest Women Often Cry Behind Closed Doors

She's the strongest person everyone knows,
A beautiful soul who always seems to be smiling and laughing...
But they know what she wants them to know, they see what she wants them to see.
She accepts and loves people for who they are, without judgement or expectation.
Her battles are the quiet ones no one knows about, behind closed doors and silent tears.
She cries from inexplicable sadness, momentary angst and absolute weariness.
Not the sort of tired that sleep can satisfy, but the deeper kind- a soulful fatigue that needs much more than rest.
She seeks no pity from those in her life, for she is the strong one...
Because sometimes, being strong is her only choice.
She loves with all her heart, lives every day to its fullest and gives everything her all.

She's learned to temper her expectations and depend on herself.

Strong willed, sassy and feisty, she's the woman that people never forget and she makes sure her voice is heard.

Not just to talk, but because her words have meaning and her thoughts matter.

She's not a candle in the wind, she's a roaring wildfire.

It doesn't mean she doesn't fight her internal battles of insecurities, fears and worry, only that she knows her strength and never gives up.

She's not a fighter because she always wins, but because she never stays down.

She's okay with being a beautiful mess and a wonderful disaster,

Because she's not defined by all the things others focus on-flaws and imperfections.

She knows who she is, what she wants and she won't stop until she's happy.

She's the strongest of women, but not in the way that people think-

She's tough in heart and hardy of soul.

She loves when she shouldn't, more than they'll ever love her back...

And yet, she still keeps pouring out her heart.

That's the beauty and blessing of a strong and soulful woman.

The Strength to Love a Broken Woman

She's never asked for help in her life, fighting the battles and making her breaks all on her own.
Sure, she's been frustrated, knocked down and counted out numerous times...
But she always found a way to get back up, rise from the ashes of her failure and keep going.
Not once did she feel sorry for herself or ask why...
She did what she had to do to survive.
And each time, after every broken heart and all the failures, she picked up her shattered pieces and figured out how to rebuild herself stronger than before.
What she learned along the way was that the world seemed more intent on focusing on her flaws than celebrating the beauty of her recovery.
They didn't see the strong and resilient woman who never stayed down...they criticized her cracks, lamented her flaws and judged her without ever knowing who she truly was...

But she soon realized the person whose opinion truly mattered was staring back at her in the mirror.
The woman she was becoming wasn't stuck looking back over her shoulder at what she had been...
She was lifting her eyes to the bright future and all that lay ahead.
While she had taken the long road to get where she was, every misstep, bad decision and mistake led her exactly where she was meant to be...
And forged her strength and armor in the process.
So, when they asked her if she'd change anything about where she'd been or what she'd been through, she'd just smile with a twinkle in her eye and say no.
She knew what they seemed to forget:
Her cracks were how the light got in, and she was determined to be the brightest light in the sky...
And there was nothing that would stop her from being happy and the most beautiful light that she could be.

She Always Finds Her Strength

She'll never tell you she has it all figured out.
She charges forth into most of her days without a clue how she'll get it all done, make it all work and find all the answers she's looking for.
But that's just the thing about this strong and beautiful woman- she'll never worry about the "how," for she will always figure it out.
That's just who she has and the bravery that life has taught her-
She was never given a choice on who she would become.
There's never been the easy path or help along the journey…
She's learned to depend on herself and that has made all the difference.
She'll tell you she makes mistakes all the time, trips and falls a time or two…but that she always manages to find her way.
So, when she climbs to the tops of the mountains she's been forced to overcome, she does so with pride and a fierce sense of accomplishment.

She did it, even when she thought she couldn't.
She beat the odds, fought back and rose harder…
That's why she knows that she can do anything if she sets her mind to it.
The only one who can defeat her…
Is her.
And that's not going to happen in her story.
She'll turn the page, start a new chapter and make a new ending...
But she'll never stay down, quit or stop trying.
She's stronger and hardier than to be that one that gives up…ever.
So if you see her on her knees, battling life and struggling to survive, be prepared to watch her rise from the ashes of a fiery battle.
She keeps showing up, keeps trying, keeps going.
She forged her strength in the fires that would have consumed anyone else…
And they just made her stronger.
So, when I tell you that she's one of a kind, make no mistake:
You'll never find another like her.
Appreciate her like she deserves.
Women like her don't come along very often.
She's amazing, just the way that she is…

She Does Whatever It Takes

She made the choice a long time ago to never surrender to the problems and challenges that tried to bring her down.
She never set out to become strong, tough or brave, her story never gave her another option.
She's always done whatever it takes to make it where she's trying to go, but she's never sold her soul or sacrificed her values to reach her goals.
She's not perfect, and she gave up trying to be a long time ago.
She's made her fair share of mistakes, wrong turns and bad love choices, but that never dissuaded her from pressing forward.
She never asked "why me," she just found a way through the struggles....every time.
She's more than just a simple woman, though you may not know that at first glance.
She's a warrior spirit, with the soul of a dreamer and the heart of a lover...

More than anything, she's been searching for peace and love since the very beginning.
She's always been that person that loves with all her heart-
Herself, her people, her life…and perhaps, one day, her "forever person," when he shows up.
She's never questioned the timing of life; she's learned to do the hardest thing of all:
Trust.
Herself, her heart, life's timing-all the things that she should have stopped believing in so long ago, but never did.
She's had her heart broken into a million pieces and she's always been the one to pick up the pieces and put herself back together again...
Each time better and stronger than before.
She's a complex person with simple needs and she's never abandoned her desire to be happy in the things that matter.
She's more than a survivor- though, some days, she felt like that was all she was doing.
Most importantly, she's always kept her fire burning and kept her light shining brightly in her eyes -always believing in herself throughout it all.
Maybe one day she'll rest and take some time for herself….but that time isn't now.
She still has much to do and an entire future full of possibilities….
Falling in love with being alive every day.
Strong, beautiful and free.

One day,
She'll be in love with herself and her life, finally at peace and content, perhaps, even more...
And she can't wait to finally be happy and rest-
She's earned all of that and more....a long time ago.

I'm Brave Enough to Seek The Life I Want

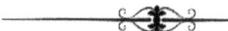

There were so many times I didn't think I would make it...
When I thought heartbreak, life or failure would finally overwhelm me.
The days when everything that could go wrong did and it took everything I had just to keep going.
People would tell me I'm strong, brave or whatever word they chose to use...
I just called it survival.
I didn't have the answers and I rarely knew the way, all I knew for sure was that I couldn't quit.
Underneath the misery and past the darkness in my life was a flickering light that kept calling to me...
It would whisper to me amidst my struggle...
"Don't give up."
Every time I wanted to throw in the towel, each time I thought I was done,
I would think of that distant light and muster up my courage to pick myself up, dust myself

off and press forward.
It was always painful and hard, never without strife and struggle, but I always found my way.
I had always lived in a constant state of fear- holding my breath waiting for the next bad thing, heartache or disappointment.
That's a tough place to live when you're always expecting disaster around every corner.
I got to a point where I just got tired... tired and fed up.
I was sick of living my life fighting for survival every day, holding onto the painful past and thinking that what I was doing would change my present or future.
All the anger, shame and guilt of where I'd been were burning me like a branding iron...
Searing the fear into my psyche that I couldn't shake, shackling me and weighing me down so heavily I could barely smile.
I hit that wall and something inside of me clicked.
I was done living afraid of what might happen, who might hurt me or what could go wrong.
It would take a long journey and many battles, but I was determined to change my mindset, my heart and free my soul.
Looking back now, I realize that choice saved my life, because my downward spiral would have consumed me whole.
Maybe I don't have the answers or even know where I'm going some days, but I know I'll end up where I'm meant to be.

I found that distant light that was calling to me for so long …it was the love for myself that was just waiting to be found.

So, yes, I started over, stumbled and fell…

But I also rose again, dug myself out and found my wings.

My life isn't perfect and won't ever be,

But with love in my heart and peace in my soul, I'm living my life and finding my love just the way I was always meant to.

For me, by me, because of me.

Beautiful, strong and free.

Today, I Rise Again

I thought I had everything under control.
Life, love, anything that came my way didn't faze me…until it did.
I believed I was strong enough to handle anything until something stronger came along.
When life brings you to your knees, you have to make a choice-
Either stay down or fight back.
There was only ever one path for me.
I spent a lot of dark nights searching my soul for the courage to dig my way out of rock bottom.
The bumps and bruises of the struggle hurt worse than anything I'd ever known-emotional scars that I'm still healing from.
But that was the catalyst for my comeback.
Pain will either make you shrink and hide...
or grow and get stronger.
So, I chose to become a warrior.
I reclaimed my power, forged new strength from the things that once tore me apart...

And I kept going.
I refuse to live my life in fear of what may happen, worry about what I can't control and shrink from the battles of life.
No, I'm choosing to rush headfirst into the challenges, growing stronger with each step and fiercer with every struggle.
Sure, I still fall down.
There are people that still hurt me.
Yes, I still cry in the shower and wipe away quick tears in the car.
I've even broken a time or two.
It doesn't get easier and the pain doesn't just go away.
I'm just strong enough now to fight my way through fiercely.
So, you may see me falling apart, but you won't see me stay down, quit or give up.
I'll do whatever it takes to overcome anything....for myself and the people I love.
Real warriors don't accept failure, and that's who I've worked hard to become.
No matter how hot the fires of life's battles may burn to try to tear me apart,
I know I can keep rising from the ashes.
I'm always going to step back from the fray...
Keep remembering who I am,
Standing strong and proud.
I Look in the mirror every day and remind myself.
"Today, I rise again."

When a Woman Is Silent

She sits there, quiet .... lost in her thoughts.
Her face shows no emotion, for her stoic facade is the face she's perfected.
She has built the incredible strength to tuck away even the fiercest emotions behind the demeanor of a steel warrior.
Her strength, built from walking through the fires of life, isn't obvious at first glance ....
No, it's made up of the quiet courage and bravery that many would probably miss about her.
But her people – the ones who love her – appreciate that about her so very much.
That's not to say she doesn't burst into tears in the shower or face down into a pillow sometimes, but she recomposes herself just as quickly, wiping away the tears and pulling herself back together.
She's a beautiful creature in her quiet virtue, able to maintain her composure when the world is crashing down around her.

She feels the same emotions you and I do, yet somehow, she's able to harness her self-control and measure her responses very calmly ....

She may overthink situations, she may be falling apart inside or on the verge of tears, but she decides when to open the floodgates of emotion to release her heart.

Not just anyone is privy to such things, for she values her time and chooses her companions carefully.

She's careful with her heart and her love, for she's been burned before and has vowed to be selective when letting her walls down.

Truth be told, there's nothing in this world as extraordinary as a strong woman ....

She fights battles few ever know and chooses which mountains to climb and which to simply walk around.

So, if she's without words, know that a myriad of emotions may be swirling inside her heart and mind.

You may not be able to fully understand who she is or how she manages a smile through hardship, but one thing is for certain:

You're witnessing one of the most beautiful people you'll ever meet as you look upon her ....

Appreciate her, cherish her, and most of all, love her for the extraordinary person she is ....

A strong and resilient woman.

The Times That Broke Me Showed Me Just How Strong I Could Be

I never wanted to be strong- I never chose the journey that I am on, it chose me.
I didn't have any idea what lie ahead of me in this life and nothing could have prepared me for the fight of my life that came my way.
I've been faced with some of the hardest battles and most difficult struggles I've ever faced....and truthfully, I don't know how I overcame it all.
There were times when I thought I couldn't go on and days that I didn't think I'd survive…
But I did, every time.
Every time at rock bottom, I managed to dig my way out and find the light.
I don't even know how I did it sometimes, but I did.
Even at my lowest, darkest place, I kept getting back up, kept rising again.

I learned more about myself in those moments than I'll ever learn during the easy times.

I found a courage that I didn't know I had and a strength I didn't think I possessed.

I did more than just survive, I fought back each time, harder, stronger and fiercer.

I became what I had to become in order to press forward and keep going.

It's not been easy and I have the scars to remind me where I've been, but I'm still here, still standing strong.

When times got hard and my life threatened to tear me apart over and again, I kept picking up the pieces of myself and reforging them...

Each time stronger and more beautiful than the last.

Looking back, I can't say that I'd ever change anything about where I've been and the person it's made me.

I know that I'm exactly where I'm meant to be and that I'm doing just what I'm supposed to be doing.

No, I don't have it all figured out, not even close.

But because of the fires that tried to burn me alive, I know who I am and what I'm capable of being, doing and overcoming...

There's now a fire burning inside of me that nothing will ever diminish.

And no one can ever take that away from me.

I'm much more than a survivor, I'm a warrior...

And with love in my heart and fire in my spirit, there's nothing that I can't overcome.

If it's to be, it's up to me...
And I've got a lot of life still to live...
So that's just what I'm going to do-
Start living my best life...
One day, one hope, one beautiful dream at a time.

I'm a Warrior, Survivor & Fighter

There are a lot of days when I get up and I have no idea how I'm going to make it through the day.
It seems that everything is stacked against me and anything that could go wrong....does.
I'm worried, I'm afraid and I doubt myself in those moments sometimes...
But somehow, those are the days when j look in the mirror and pause.
I take a deep breath, clench my fists and remind myself just who I am.
How I've survived so much to get to where I am now and how strong I've become.
I took a long look at the person I've fought to become and I smile with pride.
Most people would have quit.
Many others wouldn't have made it to where I am...
But then,
I'm not like the rest of them.

I'm a warrior with a heart of gold and the will to survive.
Maybe things don't always turn out like I want them to be, but I always get what I need when I need it and I make it work.
I'm a survivor, a scrapper, a fighter.
I pick up the pieces like I have so many times before and I figure it out.
I won't tell you it's glamorous and pretty how I get through the hard times...
But it doesn't have to be.
What matters is that at the end of the day, I'm still standing.
Maybe I'm bruised and beaten up a little bit and that's okay.
I'll regroup and recover and rise again tomorrow, renewed and determined to grow and get better.
So, that's just what I do.
And when the first light of a new day finds me, there's a smile on my face a renewed vigor in my soul.
No matter how the day goes or the challenges that face me,
I'll get through it all.
With character, strength and grace.
Most of all, I do it my way.
I've got this...and I always will.

Her Strength Is Subtle and True

She knows all the reasons to be careful with her heart, but she still loves with reckless abandon.
She knows who she is ... she's a woman who believes in love, though it drives her friends crazy that she loves more than she'll ever get back.
She takes the risks knowing the pain that often waits on the other side of love gone wrong. Nothing will dissuade her from following her heart.
She's not foolish and she's far from naive – just the opposite, in fact.
She's strong and resilient in ways most will never know, and she refuses to live or love small, because she's holding out for her forever.
She's going to kiss however many frogs it takes, turn the page of her love story as many times as she needs to so that she'll find her meant to be.
The difference between her and so many others is that she doesn't need a man at all .... though she craves fulfilling companionship, she longs to share the joys of life with her special someone.

If love never comes knocking, she'll be quite content to love herself, her friends and her life just the way it is ....

But that doesn't mean she won't give her all in pursuit of her true love.

She doesn't know anything other than passion, love and soulful depth – they're an integral part of who she is, and she'll never deny her truths or shy away from a chance to love someone.

She knows what she deserves, and she'll never settle .... but she's strong enough to handle the pain and risk that can come with romance.

Most would swear off trying, saying it isn't worth it, but she's not one of those people.

She's got a heart of gold and wears her feelings on her sleeve ....

Unafraid to plunge headfirst into the madness of love ....

Because she made herself a promise long ago that no matter how hard life tested her, what people said or the heartache she had to endure, she wouldn't give up on love.

So, she won't.

There will never come a day for her when she has to say "if only ...."

So, she may give more love than she'll ever get back, but she'll keep loving anyway.

She's strong, beautiful and believes in love ....

And she wouldn't have it another way.

She is a Woman With a Heart of Gold

She made the choice a long time ago to never surrender to the problems and challenges that tried to bring her down.
She never set out to become strong, tough or brave, her story never gave her another option.
She's always done whatever it takes to make it where she's trying to go, but she's never sold her soul or sacrificed her values to reach her goals.
She's not perfect, and she gave up trying to be a long time ago.
She's made her fair shares of mistakes, wrong turns and bad love choices, but that never dissuaded her from pressing forward.
She never asked "why me," she just found a way through the struggles, every time.
She's more than just a simple woman, though you may not know that at first glance.
She's a warrior spirit, with the soul of a dreamer and the heart of a lover...

More than anything, she's been searching for peace and love since the very beginning.
She's always been that person that loves with all her heart-
Herself, her people, her life…and perhaps, one day, her "forever person," when he shows up.
She's never questioned the timing of life, she's learned to do the hardest thing of all:
Trust.
Herself, her heart, life's timing-all the things that she should have stopped believing in so long ago, but never did.
She's had her heart broken into a million pieces and she's always been the one to pick up the pieces and put herself back together again…
Each time better and stronger than before.
She's a complex person with simple needs and she's never abandoned her desire to be happy in the things that matter.
She's more than a survivor- though, some days, she felt like that was all she was doing.
Most importantly, she's always kept her fire burning and kept her light shining brightly in her eyes…always believing in herself throughout it all.
Maybe one day she'll rest and take some time for herself…but that time isn't now.
She still has much to do and an entire future full of possibilities…
Falling in love with being alive every day.
Strong, beautiful and free.

One day,
She'll be in love with herself and her life, finally at peace and content, perhaps, even more...
And she can't wait to write the best chapters of her life.

From Broken to Beautiful

She's the one that scares off all the men-she is everything they want yet they have no idea the truth that lies behind her eyes.
They don't know how to approach her nor what to make of her....she's something rare, beautiful and dangerous to them.
They'll say she is difficult, hard to please or stubborn, but the reality is that she has standards, she's guarded and doesn't settle.
The weaker men will call her the things she isn't because it makes them feel bigger and stronger...
Not because any of it is true.
She doesn't need their approval or permission to be who she wants to be....she never has and never will.
In fact, she'll never need a man, because she's learned she can do anything she needs herself.
She knows that a strong man will not only understand her but will appreciate her as well...
He'll be enraptured by her strength, enamored by her spirit and love her heart...

And that's all she really wants:
Passionate love, soulful connection, and an appreciation of who she is...
But she will never sacrifice her self-respect, her heart or her integrity for anyone.
She'll never love a man trying to tame her, because she yearns to find the one that can run with her.
She won't chase love or attention any more, those were always the pursuits that broke her heart the worse.
If they can't accept her on her terms, she'll just walk away...
She'll never compromise who she is for someone to love her.
The most powerful truth of her is that she doesn't need love...she is content and complete without seeking her love story.
She'll find it when the time is right, but she won't worry about what's meant to be ...because she learned to focus on what she can control- herself.
She knows she isn't easy to love, that she keeps parts of herself guarded, because she's been hurt before and vowed to never again allow someone to destroy her.
Her walls are the highest, but her love is the deepest- she realizes that any man wanting to love her will require patience, empathy and most of all, soulful love.
She's wild and beautiful, not a creature that will ever be controlled or confined.

The one meant for her will get that about her and most of all, he will encourage and support her dreams and desires.
She knows she's not for the faint of heart, her fiery love isn't just for anyone...
but the strongest will find her fire irresistible.
So, until she meets the one who can run with her and loves her burn in only the way her soulmate can,
she'll keep doing what she does best:
Live wild, love hard and always...
She'll enjoy the moments of her life...
Independent, strong and free.

The Strongest Women Are The Hardest to Catch

She's rebuilt herself from broken hearts, broken roads and broken dreams.
She didn't have an easy past that led her to today, just the opposite.
She's fought, clawed and battled bravely to become the woman she wants to be ....
Never settling, never quitting, never losing hope.
She's more than just one of a kind, strong and resilient, and she's not one who will accept being treated disrespectfully or as just another option.
In fact, she's holding out for a love of the highest caliber – not because she needs companionship or love, but because she wants a love worth having.
One that will see her for who she is, what she's struggled to become and appreciate her .... all of her.
She's experienced all the wrong kinds of love, and she promised herself that she was done letting undeserving people try to take up space in her heart.

People would tell her not to risk her heart for love because it never works out for anyone, but she shakes that off ....

She believes that true love exists, and she won't give up hope.

She refuses to sacrifice her morals, settle for anything less than the best or most of all, tolerate lackluster passion .... in herself or the ones close to her heart.

She knows her worth, loves herself and believes she can conquer the world on any given day.

Sure, she still has days that try to bring her down, but she's always going to be stronger than the worst storms that life throws at her.

So, when you cross her path, you won't ever forget seeing a woman of her quality.

She's proud, brave and strong in all the ways you may never know ....

But that's what makes her more than an everyday woman, much more than a one-of-a-kind person, but rather an immeasurable once-in-a-lifetime soul ....

She's not an everyday woman, and she'll never be okay with just an ordinary love ....

And she shows up every time with a smile on her face, a fire in her heart and passion in her soul.

That's the mark of an amazing woman.

Beautiful, strong and free.

She is and will always be ....

Unforgettable.

I Changed It All

It took me a long time to get to a point where it was just fed up with my life...
But once I got sick and tired with everything , I knew I had to change my life or spend the rest of my days frustrated...
And I'm not going to live that way...ever.
I've worked too hard and paid the price too many times to let things turn out the way they've been going.
I'm letting go of the toxic people, dead end relationships and fake friends.
I need more authenticity and genuine connections in my life...
And that all starts with me.
I don't care anymore about what's cool and trendy, I have my own style and that's what is important to me.
I'm no longer letting people disrespect and disregard me or my feelings.
I'm taking a stand for who I am, what I deserve and what I want.
If my life is to change, it's up to me.

I know it'll take a bit of bravery, a tad of courage and a whole lot of determination…
But I'm up to the task.
This is my life and I don't want to look back and regret that I didn't do more, change more and become more.
I've got one shot at this and I'm not letting myself down.
It'll be an uphill battle to get myself and my life to where I want to be,
But I'll get there.
Life isn't a race, it's a journey...
And I'm stepping up my game and letting go of what I have been to become what I can be.
This is my time and my choice...
So I'm choosing change.
One day, one challenge and one dream at a time.
I'm allowed to be a masterpiece and a work in progress at the same time...
And that's just what I am-
I couldn't love that and myself more.

My Story Chose Me

I never really had a choice on the person I became.
I went down all the broken roads and fell down so many times, I didn't know if I would ever get back up sometimes.
When you find all the doors closing and feel disappointment around every corner, you almost stop seeing the good things in your life.
It's easy to get stuck in all the bad stuff and even easier to wallow in it.
I had a choice...
Either stay in the darkness and accept being miserable, or choose to rise above the struggle and forge an iron will that can't be broken.
Yes, my wings got clipped for a time.
Yes, I stumbled and fell to my knees.
Yes, I stopped being happy for a while...
But that's when I remembered who I was and that I was so much more than I had let myself become.
I'm not a failure even though I've failed.
I've made mistakes but that will never define me.

I'll stumble and fall, but I won't stay down- ever.
I found myself in a black abyss that threatened to overwhelm me.
However, that's not my story.
Yes, it's one of heartbreak and struggle, a tale of failure and setbacks, but my story is so much more than that.
It's also full of chapters of fighting back, finding my strength and rising from the ashes.
While I can't go and change the mistakes of the beginning, I hold the power to rewrite the next chapters and create a happy future.
It may not be the prettiest tale of adventure, love and dreams, but it will always be genuine, authentic and real...
Just like me.
Forget all the negativity that once dragged me down, I'm forging a different direction.
One full of hope, love and dreams that will resurrect my spirit in ways that once, I didn't think possible.
I know now what I never realized before:
I control my own destiny and it's up to me where I end up and how.
Now, I'm raising my voice, stoking my passion and spreading my wings like I never did before.
This time, I'm reaching for the stars and never looking back.
My life, my dreams.
Just like me, they're absolutely strong
and immeasurably beautiful.

I Got This

I only wanted to be happy, that's all I set out to find.
I didn't have a plan other than to listen to my heart and chase my dreams.
But, I didn't end up where I planned to go, but I did arrive exactly where I needed to be.
I didn't choose to be strong....that never even crossed my mind.
Sometimes, you find your strength when being strong is your only option.
I stumbled and fell flat on my face so many times I wondered often if I should even keep getting back up.
But that's just who I am-
I have fire in my veins and embers in my heart and I always will.
I don't know how to quit and I'll never stay down for long.
I don't care what brings me to my knees, I will always stand back up and keep moving forward.
Truth is, I have been broken more often than I care to admit, but that was exactly what I needed to let the light into my soul.

My true strength isn't how I kept from breaking, but how I kept going after I broke.
I don't have the answers and most times,
I'm a beautiful disaster that is lucky to match socks or remember what day it is.
The most wonderful part?
I don't have to have it all together, because I never truly will...
I like to say that's part of my charm.
So, for anyone looking for perfect, then don't look to me if that's what you want.
I'm beautifully broken, but amazingly awesome and always genuinely authentic .
And oh yes, I'm also impossibly strong.
So, if you're looking for me,
You'll find me out dancing in the rain and embracing the hurricane.
I may not be everything you've ever hoped for, but I'll always be real, authentic and true...
and maybe exactly what you never knew you always needed.
Mind, spirit and soul,
I'm strong in all the ways that matter.
So now, every time life tries to bring me to my knees, looks me in the eye and tells me...
"You can't withstand the storm,"
I simply smile back and say...
"I am the storm."

I Will Not Change Who I am

I tried for the longest time to fit in, follow the crowd and conform to what everyone else thought I should be...
And I realized that I'd never be happy that way.
Seeking approval or permission isn't something I can do anymore.
That's the kind of happy I can't live with it.
I need my own expression of who I am and how I want to live...
Whether it's how I dress, what I say or even the snorts that sneak out when I laugh.
I'm uniquely and beautifully me and if you can't appreciate me for all of my sometimes loud, often times outspoken personality, then that's your choice.
I'm not for everyone and I'm okay with that.
I need to like and love myself most of all, so that's the choice I made a while ago...
And it set me free-
To make my own decisions, to listen to my heart and fulfill my soul.

No more caring what everyone else thinks about who and what I should be.
I'm me and the people that love me love that.
I'm never going to wake up one day and realize that everyone likes me but me.
Forget that.
Life is too beautiful to be unhappy.
No pretending or make believe.
I'm uncommonly real, daringly genuine and always authentic.
I love hard when I do and I immerse myself in the moments of my life that make me feel alive.
Because this is my life and I'm living it in such a way that I'll never have regret, guilt or feel empty that I didn't chase my dreams or seek to fulfill my purpose.
So, if you're looking for me, you'll find me out there, flying by the seat of my pants, being myself in a uniquely beautiful way that no one will ever forget...
Most of all, I'll truly love me...
Because at the end of my days, I will always look in the mirror and know that I gave every day and every moment my all.
I am who I am...
And I love that person.
It's up to you if you want to do the same.
I'll still by flying high and shining brightly.
Just being me.
Take my hand if you want to join me on this amazing ride called life.
We've got a lot of living to do...

.Sometimes I Don't Want To Be Strong Sometimes, the world just gets a bit too much for me and I have to step back and take a deep breath.

All the expectations and things to do can get overwhelming...

And that's when I remind myself that I'm just one person and that the storms and busyness will pass.

That I don't have to try to be everything for everyone all the time...

Even as I want to be the strong one that anyone can depend on, that defies the odds and seems to able to overcome any challenge...

Even I need to rest sometimes.

It's hard for me, but I have to remember that it's okay not to be okay, to be tired...even to be not strong.

I have to step back and remind myself to live in the moments more- to be fully present and enjoying life as it comes.

Putting away the to do lists, to stop looking at my calendar and start seeing the beauty all around me.

I have to be able to admit that sometimes, I'm not okay.

I'm a messy bundle of nerves that doesn't have all the answers and worries more than I should...

It's okay not to always be okay.

It doesn't matter what the world expects or demands....it matters most what I want, what I can do and just being happy.

Loving passionately, living fully and laughing heartily...

Being outside the box that everyone tries to put us into with their expectations, demands and definitions.
No, I think I'm going to start doing more of the things that make me happy, fill my heart and bring joy to my soul.
Maybe I'll start stealing away from my day every so often and finding some time to let out frustration, breathe deeply and just "be" for a bit.
There's always going to be storms, bad days and things to do...
But I can start taking care of me more.
If I don't, no one else will, either.
Life is a journey, not a sprint, so I'm going to slow down, enjoy the moments and be happy when I can.
I won't always be okay, be strong or be perfect…
But I don't have to be.
So long as I'm the best and truest version of myself, the rest of it will work itself out...
I'll make sure of it.
I'm many things- imperfectly beautiful, a gorgeous mess and most of all, real.
I'll keep doing the best that I can and that's enough.
One moment, one day and one beautiful dream at a time.
It's all up to me.
I'm going to keep choosing happiness.

She Will Always Say "I Got This" with Tears in Her Eyes

She's not had an easy life- life has shattered her into pieces more often than not...
But she has always found a way to get back up, fight back and rise against the challenges that threatened to sweep her under the tides of life.
There were many times when she didn't know how she'd survive the day or get things done, but somehow, some way, she always has found her way through the hardest things.
That's who she is- fighter, survivor, protector, doer of all the things that her people need her to be and do.
For her, it's not a question of "if" or "how."
She doesn't have the time or energy to worry about the things she can't control, so she pours herself into becoming the strongest and most unstoppable person that she can be.
She rests when she can, sleeps when she must and always....just keeps going.

Others marvel at her tireless energy and her never fail attitude, but what they haven't seen or don't know is the price she's paid to forge the strongest will in life's harshest fires.

Nothing has ever come easy, and she's been challenged every step of the way...

And still, she remains undaunted by the struggles that rage across her life.

She's more than a survivor, she's an iron warrior with a heart of gold.

She loves passionately, lives intensely and will never accept failure as an option.

But there will always be those quiet times that the world will never see-

When this fierce woman breaks down, cries and falls apart, even if for the briefest of times....it's when she collects herself and gathers her strength.

Maybe it's in the shower or when she pauses to inspire herself at the start of a day.

But just as quickly as the tears fall, she composes herself and sparks that fire that fills her veins.

She's fine, she's always fine...she'll always be fine.

Even when she says "I got this" with tears in her eyes...

Because she does and always has found her way.

She wasn't born a warrior, but she learned to forge her strength in the flames of life...

She never had another choice.

She didn't just walk through the fire, she became it...

Strong, proud and fierce-

Not what she meant to become,
But who she ending up being…
And she loves every bit of the woman
She's fought so hard to be.

She'll Gather the Best of Her and Then She'll Simply Walk Away

She's fallen apart before, so this time is no different. She'll pull herself together, pick up the pieces she needs and begin to rebuild herself like she always has.
Broken hearts and lost loves are no stranger to her, she's waded through the seas of her discontent many times before.
It's the risk she knows she faces when she chooses to love, for she loves with all her heart and gives it her all.
She doesn't do anything halfway and passion fills her soul as she seeks love ....
So, as she picks up the shattered pieces of her heart, she knows this lonely road all too well.
It aches to her deepest places, but that's the price she's accustomed to paying for loving the way she does .... and she wouldn't change a thing about who she is and the choices she makes.

She'll never stop believing in happily ever after and true love, so she long ago made peace with the road to happiness.

She learns something from every dead end and tries to grow each time.

She'll pick up the pieces she needs to move on and move up, leaving behind the parts of the past that don't serve her anymore ....

She knows that to truly evolve, she must let go of the baggage that used to weigh her down and open the doors to new possibilities.

Her friends tell her she's strong and brave, not that she sees that in herself.

She just sees a woman with a broken past trying to build a brighter future as she picks up the pieces along the way to forge her armor.

She didn't choose this path, for she had no other choice ....

She just kept pushing forward, kept believing, kept loving like she does.

So, when the darkness of broken love tries to bring her down, she shrugs it off and keeps moving.

She knows this challenging road .... and nothing on it will ever bring her down.

Living, laughing and loving with all her heart will always be her way ....

And as she picks up the pieces from a lost love, she just smiles and laughs.

"Not today, sadness .... not ever."

With one last look, she shakes her head and turns her face to the sunlight.
Some souls were just meant to shine brighter .... so that's exactly what she kept doing ....
brighter than the night sky.

Love Yourself Deeply with the Same Passion with Which You Love Others

For so long I spent every bit of my heart on the people that I loved.
I love my people deeply because that's who I am .... and that's not going to change.
But I never realized that I while I was using all of my energy on everyone else, I never left anything for myself.
I would always put others before myself because I'm a person who loves to see others happy.
But those same friends helped me understand that I deserve that same love too ... that I was worthy of loving myself in a way that I had ignored for too long.
Truthfully, it's easier to avoid parts of yourself when you're focused on others ....
And when I chose to give the best parts of me to me, I came face to face with my own truths – some wonderful and some not as pretty.

I had to confront the things I had ignored, avoided and even buried as I projected my focus onto others. I'll never change my giving heart, but I know now that I must love myself first .... all of me, or I'm lying to myself and not being honest.

Oh, I know it's not always going to be easy, and there'll be days when I don't want to face it. But that's just part of my journey.

There's only one way through the pain and the past, and it's straight through.

I'll stumble and fall, cry in frustration and want to pull my hair out, but I know this is the only way I will ever be able to truly love all of myself the way I've always deserved.

More than that, I can love my people and my partner with a greater passion than I've ever had … a love born of peace and letting go.

So, here's to making peace with the pain, finding a way through the hard stuff and learning how to finally love myself fully.

It may be messy and harder than I realize, but I can do this.

With love in my heart, fire in my soul and an iron will, There's nothing that I can't do.

She Will Rise

I never had one of those lives where I could take it easy and just relax.
While everyone else could sit back and enjoy the ride, I had days full of challenges and nights full of struggle.
There wasn't time to rest or the chance to do what I wanted...
For as long as I can remember, my life has been a journey of fires and storms.
Fires that tried to consume me and storms that were intent on drowning me...
None of that ever stopped me, it only made me stronger.
There were many times that I was forced to my knees fighting for survival in a world that seemed determined to bring me down...
But each time, I got up, dusted myself off and found a way to keep going.
No one ever gave me much of a chance to make it, but then, I don't need anyone's approval or permission to be the independent, strong and empowered person that I am.

I'm not the one who will ask for help because I've never had anyone helping me during the hardest times of my life.

I've had to fight, battle and scrap every step of the way for everything I have.

So, I definitely don't need to be fixed, saved or completed and I'm not holding out for a hero.

I learned a long time ago that no one was showing up to bail me out of the hard stuff…so I did what I had to do and became the hero of my own story.

Maybe I don't have a fancy costume or have a made up name, but i do have a superpower:

I'm fiercely unstoppable, each and every day.

That doesn't mean I don't get knocked down, that doesn't mean I don't have bad days...

But I don't stay down and I'll never give up.

So, all the times that the world and life tried to break me?

All that did was make me stronger, wiser and better.

Now, thanks to all the people that hurt me, all the days that shattered me and all the times that I failed, I know that I can do anything and overcome the obstacles that crash into my life.

I'm more than just a person, a brave heart and iron spirit.

I am a strong woman....and there's nothing I can't do.

I Will Never Apologize for Who I am

There comes a time when you realize that not everyone is going to like you.
Sometimes, they may dislike you for no reason, and there's nothing you can do.
Whatever their motivations are - jealousy, unhappiness or personal challenges - realize that it's not you.
It's not really you that they dislike, but themselves.
You can't fix other people nor should you try to.
Empower yourself each and every day to be the best you that you can be...
that's all you can do, all you can control.
Stop and take a deep breath.
You're never going to be everyone's favorite person, and trying to please everyone will lead to your unhappiness.
Be real, be yourself and always be authentic.
Celebrate your uniqueness and invigorate your passions.

It's better to be disliked for being genuine than to be loved for being fake.
Love your people who accept and appreciate you…walk past the rest.
Life is full of people trying to be what they aren't to get things they don't need to impress people that don't matter.
You've got one life, make it count.
There is no dress rehearsal.
Do it your way, with your style and let your voice be heard.
Who you are and what you do may not matter to everyone else, but it will always matter to those who love you…
And most of all, yourself.
If you are going to make ripples,
you might as well create waves.
You were born for greatness...
Own it, love it and let your light shine.
This is your time-
Spread your wings.
Take the chance to fall in love with being alive, every day.
You don't ever have to apologize for being amazing...
It's your time to shine, my darling,
So light up the night.
Live passionately, love intensely and always be unforgettably you.

Build Her Up

She battles every day for everything and
everyone in her life- it's just who she is.
She takes on the world and comes out on top,
still smiling, still strong.
But underneath the scratched armor and sometimes
battered exterior is a warm and gentle soul with a
heart of gold willing to help anyone.
She steps up because that's just who she is.
She doesn't need fanfare or praise, for the
happiness of others and feeling of a life
well lived is her reward.
If you have someone like her in your life,
reach out and let them know they are
appreciated, loved and important.
She might be having an extraordinarily hard
day or not feeling like herself for whatever
reason...and your words might make
all the difference.
She's not ever going to be the one who admits
weakness, needing a break or asking for help,
but just some simple words of appreciation
could mean so much.

She does what she does and is who she is because that's what she chooses- she
doesn't need anyone to make her feel
good about her choices.
But even the strongest among us get tired.
Even the fiercest warriors deserve kindness .
She's always going to be the strong woman able
to conquer any challenges- and she'll do it
with amazing bravery and spirit.
But next time you see her, just smile and
tell her she's loved and appreciated.
She's more than worth that...
She's worthy of everything.
Make sure you tell her that.
Sometimes it helps her not to feel like she's
alone against the world and that she matters
more than just because of what she does,
But simply because of who she is.

She Became Her Own Hero

She'd been told all her life to wait for her person, that love would change her life and make everything better.
The thing is, it never really worked out the way she was told.
She was looking for love and found something very different.
She sought respect, communication and effort, but instead, discovered deceit, laziness and disrespect.
She was tired of the games and just couldn't spend any more of her time and energy chasing ideals she couldn't seem to find.
She didn't need to be saved, completed or fixed- she just wanted to be loved.
So, she did what she had to do and changed- Herself, her mindset, her life and her focus.
She had fallen flat on her face as she searched for love and happiness- clinging desperately to the heartbreak of rock bottom and started trying to find her way in a world determined to destroy her.

But a curious thing happened in the fire of her struggles that brought her to her knees..
She forged a courage and strength that lifted her out of the ashes and pushed her to evolve.
It was only at her most broken that the light finally began to make its way into her soul-.the same light that illuminated the path for her to better places.
She still stumbled and fell, made some bad choices and messed things up at times..
But she learned, she grew and she evolved.
She would never have found her answers in love and her journey to become who she was meant to be was a solo tale.
She was determined to become the best version of herself as she fought, struggled and battled her way through life.
She knew that luck and chance weren't real things- everything happens for a reason.
This journey was always hers- to understand who she was and learn to love herself and it was the hardest thing she had ever done.
And that thing called love that all the stories waxed on about?
It would happen in its own time, so she put that out of her mind and began to turn her love inward.
Maybe she'd find love, maybe not.
Regardless, she'd find the love for herself that she had always wanted and the way she saw it,
That's all she could ever ask for..

In her fairy tale, the princess saved herself and built her own castle.

I Define Me

All my life, people told me that I wasn't good enough and that I got what I deserved.
I was judged by those who didn't know me and made to feel like I wasn't worth anything.
They'd have me believe that I'd never be happy and that I should accept the love of whoever I was lucky enough to find that would love me.
They couldn't have been more wrong..
they don't know me and definitely don't know what I deserve.
That ends now.
I'm taking back my power and I'm changing my path.
I know who I am and what I want and I'll accept nothing less.
I am good enough, I am worth it and I do deserve to be happy.
I'm standing up and letting my voice be heard, telling the rest of them that I don't care what they think.
They don't know my struggle- they don't know where I've been or what I've overcome,
They don't get to define me or my worth.
I'm going to find the beautiful people that will love me unconditionally, the partner who will respect me

unequivocally and the dreams that I will never let go of.

This is my time and my choice, and I choose to be more.

More than what everyone else said I could be, more than I've ever been before.

I may not have all the answers and I'll still stumble and fall, but I'll always do it by my own terms.

I've failed but I'm not a failure.

I've been broken, but I'm still beautiful.

I've been lost, but I'll find my way.

They scorned me because I was different, and I don't really care- now, I'm celebrating my uniqueness.

I'm authentic, I'm real and I'll always speak my mind.

I'm not taking the easy road and I know that it'll be challenging, but nothing worth having comes without struggle.

I know I'll have to kiss a few frogs before I find my love, and I'm okay with that.

Once in a lifetime love won't just happen without work and patience -

But I won't settle, I won't quit and I'll never accept anything less than the best.

I'm worth all the love and so much more.

I'm more than "enough,"

I'm amazing.

Just watch me while I go and change the world, one heart at a time..

Starting with my own.

She Was Always Different

She was always the one that everyone called different.
They didn't understand her and they didn't try to.
Her story was filled with quiet days and lonely nights, being cast aside by the people who just thought she was weird.
Sure, she'd always been quirky, unique and had her own style, but that's who she was.
She didn't ask anyone to like her, and she just walked away from the whispers about her "strangeness."
While the others spent their time fretting about how to conform best, she embraced her individuality and uniqueness.
It was hard, sometimes, being the one that everyone left out, but she learned long ago how to make peace with the struggles that accompanied being one of a kind.
She'd rather be marching to her own beat than following the crowd.

There was no joy for her in being the one who always did her own thing, but she was a woman of principle that would die an original than live as a copy.

She knew, as surely as the sun rose and set, that one day, the very same ones who mocked her quirky authenticity would celebrate those exact things about her..

That was how she made it through the long nights and kept her resolve high..

And one day, when she opened her door to a sheepishly smiling young lady, her heart smiled...

People were finally wanting to be her friend- because some, perhaps only a few, appreciated her strength to stand alone and her individuality.

She wouldn't treat them as they did her- she was better than that.

She would embrace the ones that welcomed her friendship and loved her for who she was.

Her kindness, loving heart and deep soul were the qualities that helped her rise above the feelings of never being accepted before.

They sought her out now for the very qualities that were once scorned..

And she showed them that only love can drive out hate..

In a world full of dandelions, she was and always would be a beautiful rose.is.

I'm A Fighter

I've fought all the wrong battles for all the wrong people who never really cared about me the way I deserved.
I kept fighting when they stopped, leaving me holding the pieces of my broken heart and wondering why I held on so long when they wouldn't.
Because I'm a fighter and I always have been.
It's in my blood, forged by the hard times that tried to take me down more than once..
But I had to learn the hard way who and what is worth fighting for and who will never stand beside me through the storms.
I want that one brave soul willing to hold my hand when things get hard, life gets tough and doesn't leave.
The one that looks me in the eye and tells me they love me and then backs it up.
People have tried to tell me I expect too much, but I know what I'm worth and what I deserve..
And I'm never going to settle, lower my standards or be okay with less.

Call me feisty, stubborn and spirited and I'll just smile and say "thank you."

In my world,

When you fight for what you want, stand up for what you believe and stay true to yourself and your values, that means something.

So that's what I'm going to do because that's who I am.

So, if you're standing before me asking me to let you love me, be sure you know what you're getting into.

I'm a handful some days while I'm a mess on other days, but I'm always real.

I'm always genuine, strong willed and loyal..

And I expect the same in return.

No lukewarm passion, halfway love or weakness lives long in my world.

So, when the winds of challenge threaten to blow us apart- and they will- are you strong enough to stand up and fight?

Strong Wom en Never Settle

She wasn't strong because she wanted to be, but because she didn't have any other choice.
When she was at her lowest point, all she could see was the anguish around her heart..
All she felt was the pain from the broken promises and people that walked away.
Her soul was weary and her heart had gotten heavy, and she knew she had to dig her way out of the darkness.
She didn't know where she'd find a light or even which direction to head, only that she wouldn't give up until she found peace.
She was tired of being sad and broken-hearted, weary of the people that tried to trample her heart for their own pleasure.
No more weakness, no more lies.
She vowed to surround herself with authentic people, the ones she could count on when she needed them most.
She'd rather have five close friends than countless fair weather people..
Her life was too precious to spend any time convincing other people to love her on her terms.

She knew her worth and wouldn't settle any more for the ones who didn't make her a priority.
Her kind voice and loving soul was but a sliver of the depth of her amazing person, one that she intended to lock away until someone could see past her pain..
The one who could speak to her soul...
The lost half of a broken circle that was her.
She didn't need to be fixed, completed or saved.
She just wanted to be loved, on equal terms with respect and passion for the remainder of her days.
Her wants weren't extravagant or demanding, but her standards were.
She loved fiercely and was loyal to a fault- she expected the same from her loved ones and partner.
She'd been down the broken road too many times to count, and perhaps she'd travel there some more, but she was done chasing love and affection.
A gentleman wouldn't expect her to chase him, and more importantly, he wouldn't let her.
Come what may, she'd never be anyone's "maybe."
This time, she was holding out for forever.

Her Courage is Her Crown

She's always had to fight for everything- she was never given anything in her life..
Not even a chance.
She was forced to scrap, claw and battle for everyone and everything she always wanted, and more times than not, it broke her.
In fact, she often felt like she spent her time constantly healing, rebuilding and growing stronger.
She'd look around and see how others were given opportunities and sometimes, it made her envious and a little sad that she, too, wasn't given anything like that.
Why wasn't her path easier like the others?
But life had bigger plans for her- a future that she could never have imagined.
The most beautiful things in life aren't always given..they're earned.
Her dreams were big and her spirit was fierce and that's exactly why she was never handed the easy stuff.

She needed to first forge her strength and courage in the flames of struggle..
So that's just what she did, though she never knew what lie in store for her..
Only that she wanted and needed more from her life than mediocre and average.
Her passion didn't allow her to do anything half way, and when she loved, she poured every bit of her heart into someone..
Leading to oft broken hearts and lost friendships, because not everyone understood her intense passion..
And they didn't have to.
She was never looking to be saved, she was determined to build herself a life and a fire that no one could ever vanquish.
She became all the things she needed to realize her aspirations-
Fighter, survivor, loyal friend, confidant, lover, dreamer.
She had a vision of what she wanted her life to become and who she wanted to be..
And she pursued that relentlessly.
No excuses, no quitting and most of all, she never stopped believing.
So, if you ever see her someday, you'll see an strong, proud woman who has earned everything she has achieved.

Don't mistake her warm kindness for weakness, for underneath the genuinely benevolent facade beats the heart of a warrior queen..
Strong, brave and fearless.
And she'll always find a way to get it all done, every day..
For this amazing woman is more than just a beautiful soul,
She wears her courage as a crown, because she is and always will be a queen.

She Learned to Get Back Up

She never had anyone to pick her back up and help her rise again when she fell.
The only person that was always there..was her.
Through the heartaches, the pain and disappointments, she didn't have anyone to turn to..and she was okay with that.
While the world sees a strong, independent woman now, there was once a broken little girl that learned never to depend on anyone.
It's not that she didn't have people to care about her, she just realized that she needed to forge her courage from the struggles of fire..
From within herself.
She always seemed to end up on broken roads chasing dead end love and trying to turn projects into partners.
She was strong enough for two people, and somehow, she inevitably tried to fix her damaged love interests.

She knew what she wanted and she wouldn't stop until she found the happiness she knew she deserved.
She stopped wasting pointless tears on people that didn't care and started loving herself for staying true to herself.
She didn't have all the answers and often got lost trying to find her way, but she didn't settle, quit or stop trying to elevate her life and find happiness however she could.
So, as she stood strong- a confident, independent and vivacious woman that amazed the world, she guarded her truths with courageous passion.
She'd make no apologies for who she was or accept treatment that was beneath her, and that didn't always sit well..
Especially with weaker people.
Come what may, she'd keep chasing her dreams, loving her people passionately and living her best life.
All those secrets that the little girl had learned to protect?
A proud woman knew that the right person would come along someday and appreciate, accept and love every one of those imperfections.
Until then, she'd keep flying high and living passionately..
In all the ways that made her happy.
And that's exactly why she was beautiful in all the ways that mattered..
Just the way she was.

She Is One of A Kind

People would look at her bold style, contagious smile and carefree attitude and shake their heads.
They never really understood her way of uniquely standing out and listening to her heart..
But they didn't have to.
She knew who she was and what made her happy ..and that's exactly what she did- go where the happiness was.
You'd often find her meandering off the beaten path, lost in the hidden beauty of the world while she sought to explore and enjoy all that life had to offer.
With her unmistakable smirk and fiery eyes, she was the wild one that couldn't be tamed, as many found out the hard way.
She believed in the things that most would scoff at, but she would never apologize for being a hopeless romantic and endless dreamer.
Her friends would try to tell her to be realistic, to temper her expectations and not to always give so much of her heart away..
But that's just who she was-
She loved hard when she did, and though she didn't fall in love easily, she wholly believed in true love and

that happily ever after was real…and that she'd have it all.

As a little girl, she promised herself to never give up on her dreams, to always believe in love and hold onto her magic fiercely.

So, maybe she was given to flights of fancy, impractical trips to nowhere and falling in love too often…

But she was always true to herself, what she wanted and lived without regrets.

She was many things, that amazing woman, but she was one of a kind.

Here today, gone tomorrow, but she left her mark wherever she went on the hearts she encountered.

So, they may have shook their heads at this free spirit given to fierce love and bold dreams, but they'd never know what it meant to live life and love passionately like she did.

Free to chase her dreams, proud to be unapologetically herself and most of all,

she would always be brave enough to keep believing in love.

Maybe she'd take the long way and get lost a time or two, but she'd always end up where she was meant to be..

And she knew that one day,

That place would be in the arms of her true love.

Until then, she would keep doing what she did best…

Live fully, love intensely and dream endlessly.

She's The Strong One

She's used to being the strong one.
She knows what it's like to be alone and facing battles that feel overwhelming.
But that's her life and she's long accepted it the way it is.
She's not going to be a victim, complain or seek help to get through her days,
For she has long known that she alone will be the one fighting for her peace, survival and sometimes, sanity.
Truly, all she seeks is happiness…
And it's often the one thing that eludes her.
But she'll keep showing up and keep trying.
That's who she is and how she is built…
Pieces together from the often broken pieces of the times that she's fallen apart and gotten back up and tried again.
Lovers have broken her heart, friends have let her down and people have disappointed her.
But she still keeps hoping and loving anyways.
She won't let the failures of the past darken her hopes for the future.

She believes in love, dreams and herself.
She fights to become the woman she wants to be.
She chooses to never give up.
She's many things, but she'll never stay in one spot and doesn't expect perfection in her life..
But she pushes herself every day to be better than she was yesterday.
Maybe someone will come along one day that doesn't try to tame her wild heart and won't seek to cage her passionate spirit,
But she hasn't found it yet…
But it doesn't mean she will give up hope.
But until that day,
She will do what she always has done.
Pick up her sword and fight the battles with unrelenting strength and fiery resolve.
She's a unique and strong woman..
And that's just what she does.
She knows the sun always rises on a new day..
So she keeps dreaming of the day when she will see the sunrise holding the hand of the one she loves.
Then, she will finally be able to rest.

She Stopped Holding Out For A Hero

She's wasted too much time hoping someone else would show up and save her...
Only to be disappointed every time.
She wanted to believe in the good of people, but when she needed help the most, none would ever arrive..
So she did what she had to do to survive-
She picked up a sword, dusted herself off and began to fight her own battles.
She was overwhelmed more often than not, knocked down and beaten up on the worst of days, but that's how she began to forge her strength in the fires of failure.
With each defeat, her armor grew stronger.
With every setback, she turned it into a comeback.
She started believing in the woman staring back at her in the mirror and stopped listening to those voices that told her she couldn't.
At her lowest point and darkest hour, she burst forth from the ashes and fought back harder than she

thought possible…
That's when she began to find her wings.
She wasn't holding out for a hero anymore.
No, she was telling her story a different way, and in her tale, she became the hero and fought her own battles.
It was gritty, real and dirty, but she always emerged on the other side, finding her way to the light.
She stopped doing just what she had to do to survive and started becoming the person she was meant to become and lifting herself up.
Maybe it wasn't always a straight line and often full of falls, stumbles and detours,
But she always ended up where she was meant to be.
And as she stood strong and felt proud at the end of a hard day, she had a strength and courage that no one could ever take away from her.
Now, when she looked in the mirror every morning, she stopped asking how she would make it through the day and said simply one thing:
"I got this."

The Woman I am Becoming

Yes, I've been down some hard roads and had some bad things happen to me in life.
I never had a choice on the path I chose-
It chose me instead.
I was once that person that didn't know how they'd make it through the days…
I used to let every bad decision, heartbreak and disappointment wreck me for days…
But I'm not that person anymore.
I had to change to survive, so that's just what I did.
I grew stronger, wiser and braver through every storm life brought down on me…
Fighting for my life to stay afloat when the tides of trouble tried to bring me under.
And each time when I thought I wouldn't be able to find a way…I did.
I transformed weakness into strength, indecision into certainty and fear into courage.
It's still a battle some days, don't get me wrong..
Only now, I know I'll battle my way through the hard stuff.

I forged the woman I became out of the fires of life and each time I fell apart, I put myself back together stronger and more resilient.

Once, I couldn't see past today to tell you what the future holds.

I still don't know all the answers or know exactly how I'll get where I want to be..

But now, I can see the path ahead much more clearly.

And with each victory, every triumph and all the success, I grow more confident.

Truthfully, I'm excited about the future in a way that I've never been.

I see the person that I'm becoming and I know that my future is full of beautiful possibilities and endless hope.

That's the light that I created during those dark days when all I wanted to do was quit.

I dug deeply, rekindled my spark and ignited my passions into a roaring fire..

And now, there's nothing that will stop me or keep me down.

It's me versus me, and I know that I can do this.

More than that, I look forward to that day, far off in my future when I look into that mirror and smile…

Because I've finally become the person that I set out to be so very long ago.

She paid the price through so many hard days and long nights..

But she kept going and never quit.

The more I think about meeting her, the bigger the smile on my face grows.
I just have one thing to say to that woman I will become tomorrow:
"I've been waiting all my life for you. Let's go chase some dreams and capture some hope."
And I can promise you one thing…
I'll never be the same or look back again.
The future belongs to me now, and I can't wait to get there.

I Know Who I am

I gave up trying to be perfect a long time ago and it was the best thing I've ever done.
Trying to please all the wrong people for all the wrong reasons was the right choice for me.
I'm never going to be flawless, and I'm not going to try to be.
I'm a wonderful mixture of moods, emotions and charisma that is absolutely lovable.
Sure, I don't know where I'm going most of the time and I don't have a clue about why I'm in the mood I'm in, but that's just part of my attractiveness.
Whether my hair and makeup is a mess- if I even remembered to wear makeup at all-or if I'm completely put together, I'm the same gritty, real and down to earth gal all the time.
I may cry at the drop of the hat or burst into laughter for no reason whatsoever, but I'm always authentic and genuine.
I own my flaws and celebrate my scars, because they tell the story of my journey, my failures and my history..
And I wouldn't change who I am or where I've been for anything.

There's a unique beauty in my brokenness and a distinct wonder in my gorgeous mess, just ask anyone who knows me.

Whoever really knows me always appreciates me for everything I am..the good, the bad and the silly.

Sure, I don't have it together all the time, but truthfully, I don't have to.

I'm fine flying by the seat of my pants and figuring it out as I go.

Maybe I get lost a time or two, but I always seem to end up where I'm meant to be.

It may not always be pretty, but it's always true..just like me.

I know who I am and what I want, and I own every step of my journey- laughter, tears and all the other stuff in between.

I may not be who I set out to be, and I may not be the model person that everyone thinks I should be, but I'm an amazing woman that loves hard, lives fully and never gives up on her dreams.

If you ask me, that's a pretty good way to be.

I Choose Me

I always believed that I should try to fit in and follow the crowd.
That being like everyone else was the thing to do..
Only I never felt good just blending in and getting lost in the crowd.
Deep down, there was this voice that told me that I was unique and would never be happy being like everyone else…
So I stopped.
I stopped dressing like them, acting like them and living my life like all the others.
It's scary stepping outside of the box and dancing to your own beat.
I realized that there a lot of people who don't like the ones who do their own thing..
And that's okay- I'm not for everyone.
I don't need approval or acceptance to be okay with who I am anymore..
And that's taken time, patience and courage to get to that point.
I wasn't accustomed to going my own direction when everyone I knew was headed the opposite way.

It took some time to stop listening to the naysayers and ignore their judgements..
But I'm getting better at it every day.
I'm finding it easier to be okay in my own skin, doing my own thing and having my own opinion and style.
I'm sure there are plenty of people who don't understand me anymore or say that I've changed..
But I've actually just started being more myself than I've ever been before.
It's a good feeling to finally be living my life the way I want without caring about what everyone else has to say about me.
I've learned to look past the people that don't get me and embrace the ones who love and support me no matter what I do.
Those are my people and I love them for it-
They celebrate my choices and uniqueness in a way that the crowd never will.
While I do feel alone sometimes, I'm never really lonely.
My friends are always just a message or phone call away.
So I've lost a lot of friends and alienated some people with my choice to be true to myself,
And I accepted a long time ago that the people that will be part of my story would stick around and they've done just that..
And they're the ones that I'll be holding their hands as I walk this journey called life.

The days may not always go my way, times may get hard and I'll still stumble and fall..
But at least I finally started doing it all..
My way.

Strong Women Don 't Settle

She knew that when people met her, they'd marvel at her strength and resilience.
They imagine that she was just born that way and everything comes easy..
And that's okay, they're welcome to think what they want, because they will anyways.
No one but her closest friends knew her journey and that's the way she wanted it to be.
The world doesn't need to know the price she paid to become a force of nature-
Her sacrifices, failures and setbacks aren't necessary for the public opinion of her..
But they are part of her story.
Her narrative is a tale of growing from a broken young girl learning to survive on her own without help from anyone.
She didn't become bitter by the rejections, disappointments and struggle..
She became better.
Each day, she learned a little more, grew a bit stronger and fought a little harder for her dreams.

She didn't ask for pity, help or sympathy..
She just found a way to always get it done.
And one day, that same little girl looked in the mirror and realized that she had become a strong woman.
A warrior, in fact, that was capable of so much more than anyone ever believed she could do.
She smiled broadly in that moment because she knew she had earned every bit of who she had become.
And the ones who wanted to doubt her?
She'd just lower her gaze and invite them to walk through the fire with her.
She had learned long ago how to walk through the fire and emerge tougher and unscathed..
So she just did what she always had done:
Keep going, keep fighting and keep winning.
She'd walk past the disrespect and dismissals of others and kept rising.
She had a life to conquer and she wasn't going to let anyone or anything stand in her way.
Success with character.
Victory with respect.
Happiness with heart.
Maybe she didn't change the world, but she knew she could always change her world…
And that's what mattered to her.
How do I know this little girl now all grown up..
The strong warrior I see before me?
She is me..
And I'm still rising.

I Can Fly

I've been ignoring what my heart has been whispering for too long..
Telling me to stop standing still.
I'm not content any more to stay in one place, not moving forward and not growing.
I've let the struggles of life tear me down so far that I didn't even know if I could get back up..
But I'm better than that, stronger than I once thought.
I've been down before and always managed to find my way, I just forgot how to pick myself up for a bit.
I'm done accepting my life to be stuck at rock bottom anymore.
Those people that hurt me and let me down don't control my path, I do.
Instead of looking back and wondering why they did what they did, I'm moving on and moving up.
Truth is, I'll never know why people that say they love you hurt you and leave, but sometimes, you have to be okay with that..
And I'm learning that, day by day.

They chose their future by not including me and now, I'm through standing still holding on to heartache and heartbreak.

Those misfortunes don't define me and I'm not letting someone who's gone keep hurting me.

I can learn the lesson without harboring the pain..and that's exactly what I'm going to do.

I'm pulling myself up out of rock bottom and I'm clawing and fighting my way back to where I should have been all along.

No more wallowing, playing the victim or being content with people walking all over me.

I'm finding my voice, raising my fist and telling the world I'm taking back my life.

I'm done trying to convince people to love me or chasing partners that don't really want to love anyone but themselves.

It's time for me to rediscover my magic and fall back in love with myself.

That's what matters most of all.

Embracing my flaws, owning my choices and confronting my fears.

Stepping out and stepping up is a hard and scary thing to do, especially when you don't know where you're going...

But I'm done being afraid of the future and the possibilities- I'm capable of so much more than I've let myself become.

That ends now.

I'm turning the page and starting fresh.. the past has nothing new to say, so I'm focused on what's ahead of me.
My life, my future and love for myself.
Anyone who can accept me for who I am and support me in my dreams, I welcome with open arms.
Forget the rest- I've listened to voices who told me what I can't do all my life.
This is my time..
To shine, to breathe free and to start loving myself..
And oh yes, darling, it's my time to fly...
And never look back

Becoming A New Person

When my life came full circle and I found myself back where I started- in the streets that had once been home with people that knew my name..
It was all so familiar, but felt like a lifetime ago in so many ways.
They all knew who I was, but not who I'd become..
They didn't know that version of me- the person I had fought to become through the storms of life.
But then, I didn't expect them to know me anymore..
And if I was honest, I knew some of them would never really understand the evolution of me.
And that's okay.
You learn from change that not everyone is meant to stay in your life.
They play their part and while you may never forget who they were,
They weren't meant to be part of the final chapters.
It was a hard truth knowing that people from a life that was once all I knew wouldn't be there in the end..
But that's just how life goes sometimes.
The ones that love you and get you always seem to find a way to be there for you, even when no one else is..

And they just stick around, always.
And your heart is better for them.
And when you change, they support you and love you all the same,
regardless of what the world thinks of the new you.
So, yeah, as I turned down the streets that I had been on countless times before,
Everything just felt different now.
A good different.
I had worked hard to grow and evolve in my life to become a person I was proud to be…
And I learned most of all,
There were parts of me that I had to let go, release and set free..
Because those were the worst parts of me that held me back, weighed me down and kept me from growing.
So as I stopped for a moment to say goodbye to the life I once called home, it was a bittersweet farewell.
Some wonderful memories, some painful remembrances, but it was someplace and something I was finally moving on from.
I don't know where tomorrow will take me but even as I'm thankful for the lessons of yesterday, it's time for me to turn the page and start a new chapter.
The future is what I make of it, and the darkness of the past no longer calls to me.
I smiled as I looked back one last time.
It's a great day to start being free.

I Will Rise As The Whole Fire

I realized a long time ago that I'm going to have bad days, hard times and that I'm going to get knocked down..
That's just how life goes sometimes..
But even though I may be brought to my knees and fall down, that doesn't mean I have to stay down.
I choose never to be defined by my failures, but instead to be driven to rise again stronger every time I fall down.
I'm not saying it's easy- turning setbacks into comebacks isn't ever an overnight or painless process.
It's going to hurt and I may hate every step of the process, but it's necessary-
For me to grow,
To evolve into the person I'm meant to become.
Even the strongest person has weak days, times when they don't feel their best or the obstacles that seem overwhelming..
But I've been down those roads before and somehow, I always managed to find my way, reignite my passions and keep pushing forward.

My fire may be extinguished as the storms of life drench me in hard uncertainty, but I'll never lose my spark for long..
Because when the rains stop and my vision clears, I'll see my way back to the top..
I'll dust myself off, find my way and each time that I dig deep,
I'll rise again from the ashes,
Brighter and fiercer than I was before..
More than just a fire, a flame or a spark.
I'll come back again as a raging wildfire,
For that will always be who I am and my legacy:
Strong, fierce and unstoppable…
Like the beautiful warrior that I am.

Brave Enough To Be Real

I used to listen to all the people telling me what I should and shouldn't be..
And truthfully, it was exhausting.
What to wear, not to wear, what to say or do..
I got to a point where I lost who I was in trying to make everyone else happy.
That's when a beautiful friend told me one day to let go of all the things I wasn't and start becoming all the things I am meant to be.
I was perplexed, confused..and relieved.
I couldn't be what everyone thought I should be and simply be happy.
That's not real and I'm not settling for everyone else's opinion of my happiness.
No, I'm better than that and I'm meant for so much more.
Anyone can be beautiful, you know?
Your hairstyle, your clothes, your outward appearance..sure, those are attractive..
But not in the ways that truly matter.

I'm leaving all that superficial shallowness behind because I want more for myself, more for my life.
Why settle for being just like everyone else ?
I'm not.
I'm stepping out of the labels and expectations and I'm blazing my own trail.
I will be beautiful in the most amazing ways that will rock a world full of fake.
I'm going to be bold, strong and confident each and every day...
In my words, in how I love and what I do.
Forget a life of merely existing.
I want to be on fire for life, love and the people I care about.
They'll tell you not to have an attitude, be opinionated or different..
So that's exactly what I plan to be:
Independent, fiery and original.
I'm going to ride the wind and chase my dreams with a style I'm happy to call my own.
I'm not borrowing, stealing or copying anyone else.
That's for the weak people who don't think for themselves.
I want to look in the mirror each and every day and know that I'm living life to the fullest-
Fiercely passionate and lovingly confident.
I'm going to do what all the others tell me that I can't do..
I'll be brave enough to be real in a world full of copies.

I'm going to redefine beauty with a courage all my own.
My life, my voice, my way.
I'm never again going to allow myself to run with the rest when I'm destined to fly high.
I don't need a spotlight, my dear..
I'll always shine from within.

I Will Always Be A Fighter

I've stopped asking "why me?" and letting the past weigh me down.
It's a hard thing to trust that everything happens for a reason and that if things don't work out, I'll understand eventually.
Yeah, I've had some tough times that really hurt and I've been at rock bottom more times than I can count..
But those experiences don't determine who I am- I do.
Choosing not to stay down, to get back up and keep moving forward has made me better, not bitter.
Because I've also had great days, big accomplishments and huge happiness.
I've learned is life is a balance of the good and bad, it's up to me to find my joy in the bad days and to relish the good times.
Life will never be perfect, it will never go just as planned and there will always be those days I just don't want to get out of bed.
But I control my own destiny and I make my own choices..
And I choose happiness.

I choose to make the best out of the bad stuff and soak in the beauty of the good moments.
I choose to learn from my mistakes, embrace my flaws and keep loving myself more every day.
I am a beautiful mosaic of all of my failures and victories, and I've learned to use my pain as fuel and motivation every day to evolve.
I may never be famous or rich, but I'll be happy..
And that's what matters most.
That I faced life head on and kept pushing forward, kept rising again and found my wings to fly higher every day..
That when it's all said and done, I'll look back and treasure the little things, know that I followed my heart,
And that no matter what,
I was truly happy.

I know life can be overwhelming sometimes, the bad stuff seems to never stop. And that's okay. You've always survived the storms that sometimes threatened to bring you under and you were the never the same afterwards. And that's what the storms are for- reminding you just how strong you truly are and that no matter what, you will always be a survivor, strong and proud. Every day, you have a choice- to stand still and feel sorry for yourself or to learn, grow and evolve.

This is your time.

Find your voice and get back up.

There's a whole world waiting for you to find your wings and fly.

Become who you were always meant to be.

Arise, strong woman.

Nothing can stop you now.

Believe.

Strong Woman Arisen
Ravenwolf

Find more love, hope and empowerment at
www.theravenwolf.com
including Ravenwolf's complete works
and quote merchandise.
You Got This!

www.ingramcontent.com/pod-product-compliance
Ingram Content Group UK Ltd.
Pitfield, Milton Keynes, MK11 3LW, UK
UKHW022235230426
12048UKWH00018BA/1274

9 798885 254427